Mathura

DISTRICT MATHURA

Mathura

A Tapestry of Art and Devotion

Pradip Bhatnagar
Sangeeta Bhatnagar
B.K. Goswami

NIYOGI
BOOKS

Published by
NIYOGI BOOKS
Block D, Building No. 77,
Okhla Industrial Area, Phase-I,
New Delhi-110 020, INDIA
Tel: 011-26818960, +91 7428978881
Email: niyogibooks@gmail.com
Website: www.niyogibooksindia.com

Editor: Anwesha Panda
Design: Anushri Gupta and Shashi Bhushan Prasad

ISBN: 978-81-19626-85-4
Publication: 2025

Every effort has been made to ensure the accuracy of the information presented in this book. The images used in this book come from either the public domain or from the public commons, unless otherwise stated.

Printed at Niyogi Offset Pvt. Ltd., New Delhi, India

We dedicate this book to

the sacred land and spiritual heritage of Braj and its people

Contents

घाट

Message from

Hema Malini

When I took up the representation of the Lok Sabha constituency of Mathura in 2014, I did not realise that a plethora of magical moments and experiences were waiting to be explored in the areas surrounding Mathura and Vrindavan. Already immersed in the charm of Krishna Kanhaiya I found it easy to accept the tales and folklore of the region not as something mythical but as a divine play being acted out even today. I am truly blessed to savour the divinity of each blade of grass and each grain of sand covering the holy land of Braj.

I was thrilled to know that Shri Pradip Bhatnagar, a distinguished civil servant, almost reflecting my sentiments on the importance of Mathura–Vrindavan, has chosen to consolidate his thoughts and bring out a photo book on Mathura with attractive photographs and informative articles. Mr Bhatnagar has a wealth of administrative experience drawn from his tenure as Commissioner of Agra Division and is eminently suited to cull out a beautiful and nuanced understanding of Mathura and Vrindavan.

Mr B.K. Goswami, a senior civil servant, brings to the joint authorship an impeccable sense of authority on tourism having been a Secretary in the Tourism department of Government of India.

The third co-author, Dr Sangeeta Bhatnagar, is a name to reckon with in culinary circles and has contributed substantially to the research section of the book. As President of Akanksha Samiti of Agra, she has traveled frequently to Mathura and Vrindavan and has first-hand knowledge of arts, crafts, festivals and cuisine of the region.

Their combined efforts in bringing out this classy illustrated volume will definitely ignite a positive response from the readers.

My best wishes to the authors.

Foreword

Braj Mandal, traditionally also known as Mathura Mandal, is a unique centre of Indian culture and civilization. This area has enriched Indian polity, economy, literature, arts etc. from the time, as far back as history can take us. In this land Vedic, Buddhist, Jain and other cultural traditions bloomed with full splendour. However, Braj attained its full glory when Sri Krishna incarnated here. So declare *gopis*, in the *Bhagavata Purana* (10.31.1). Along with the manifestation of Krishna Leelas, manifested the glory and grandeur of Braj. Due to Krishna's divine touch, the land, the river, the trees, the mountains, the birds and animals of Braj, they all became 'divinised'.

Inspired and energised by Sri Krishna and his divine consort Radharani, the cultural geography of Braj became a centre of attraction for large number of humans. Ironically, by the end of 15th century, Vrindavan, the heart of Braj, was missing from geographic and cultural memory. In the beginning of 16th century many saints and eminent persons engaged themselves in rediscovering the holy places of Braj, especially Vrindavan. This unique *seva* was led by Sri Chaitanya Mahaprabhu, through his followers the famous six Goswamis. Sri Vallabhacharya, Vitthalnath, Swami Haridas, Harivamsha and many others contributed their bit in this effort. The construction of new temples, ghats, ponds, tanks, *kunj*, greens and conservation of the existing built heritage by various dedicated individuals and institutions brought Braj to its full majesty.

The celestial beauty of Braj Mandal, spread in a circle of 84 kos (over 252 km) is enjoyed through the 84 kos Braj Yatra, very popular among pilgrims and visitors. This sacred geography was already well detailed and identified in Braja Bhakti Vilasa of Narayana Bhatt of Barsana, in the 16th century. In the later part of 19th century, F. S. Growse introduced Braj to English readers through his valuable *Mathura: A District Memoir*. In the 20th century, Alan Entwistle described Braj in his well-researched *Braja: Centre of Krishna Pilgrimage*, which compliments and completes the work of Narayan Bhatt.

Braj, with Mathura–Vrindavan in its centre, draws crores of pilgrims and visitors annually. While the above mentioned books are valuable for those who want to study Braj's history and culture in great detail, there is a need for an easy introduction to the area, its history, heritage, art, culture and spirit that can connect today's visitors to Braj. Scholarly written, illustrated with lively photographs of monuments and events, beautifully produced, the publication of *Mathura: A Tapestry of Art and Devotion*, meets this requirement. This book will open the doors to Braj for those who have not been here. It will be a companion to those who are visiting Braj. For their labour of love, I congratulate the authors Sri B.K. Goswami, Dr Sangeeta Bhatnagar and Sri Pradip Bhatnagar.

Acharya Shrivatsa Goswami

Introduction

In the 10th chapter of *Srimad Bhagavad Gita* Sri Krishna reveals,

'Aham atma gudakesha
sarva-bhutashaya-sthitah
aham adish cha madhyam cha
bhutanam anta eva cha'

'O Arjun, I am seated
in the heart of all living entities.
I am the beginning, the middle and
the end of all beings.'

Lord Krishna was not exaggerating because even in human incarnation his life was a celebration. His divinity accommodated the ordinariness of the ordinary and glorified the glorious. He was a man in love and a God in his compassion. There was excitement of triumphs and setbacks of some tragedies in the endless variety of his life. Krishna's life and legend is an open book, yet there is an enigmatic quality about it; as if it is inviting you to explore and discover more.

This enigma led us to Mathura–Vrindavan, the birthplace, the playground and the karm-bhumi of the God. There we sought and found the answers to Krishna's claim, 'I am seated in the heart of all living entities'.

It has been sheer pleasure writing this illustrated volume along with my co-authors Sangeeta and Pradip Bhatnagar. They have both spent considerable amount of time visiting places connected with the Krishna lore, making frequent trips to temples, ashrams, ghats and museums in Mathura and Vrindavan. Their attention to detail was extremely productive when they researched documents. This book would not have been possible without their hard work and support.

A tribute to the many splendours of Lord Krishna will be incomplete if it does not reach people in the language he enchanted them with. We hope to bring out a Hindi version of the book in the near future.

B.K. Goswami

श्रीकृष्णद्वार
GATE No.1
श्रीकृष्ण जन्मभूमि
GATE No.1
GATE No.1

History of Mathura

According to legend and popular belief, Mathura is several thousand years old. It was in existence during the *Dwapar Yug*, the age in which Lord Krishna lived and the Mahabharat battle was fought. The Mahabharat, in which Krishna was a pivotal figure as the charioteer of Arjuna, was written around the 3rd century BCE. The events described in the Mahabharat have been placed by experts as having taken place around the 8th century BCE. Mathura, the city of Lord Krishna's birth and Braj, its countryside, have thus been in existence for atleast 3000 years.

Mathura was not, however, always a centre of Hinduism. It has a significant Buddhist and Jain history as well. As per belief, after Krishna left for Dwarka, Mathura was taken over by Jarasandh, king of Magadha. When Magadha became the centre of Buddhism under the Mauryas (322–189 BCE), Mathura too became a Buddhist city and remained so for several hundred years. Documentary proof of this comes from the writings of the Chinese travellers Fa Hien and Huen Tsang.

Page 15: Statue of a goddest excavated in Mathura. The mottled red sandstone used is typical of the Mathura School of Art.

Fa Hien visited Mathura around 400 CE and stayed for a month. He records the presence of 3000 Buddhist monks lodged in 20 monasteries as well as the existence of 6 stupas located on the banks of the Yamuna. He specifically records that the entire population from the highest to the lowest were staunch Buddhists. Some 250 years later around 645 CE, Huen Tsang corroborated much of what Fa Hien wrote, but added the existence of temples of Hindu divinities. This, according to historians, was an indication of a gradual decline in the influence of Buddhism, coinciding with the ascent of Hinduism in the 4th–6th century CE under the Gupta dynasty.

13-feet-high statue of a Jain Tirthankara excavated from the Kankali mound on display in the Jain Museum, Mathura

Archaeological proof of Mathura's past comes from discoveries made by the British in the 19th century. In 1853,

Ongoing excavation of the Kankali Mound, circa 1889

Alexander Cunningham, the first Head of the Archaeological Survey of India (ASI), discovered remnants and ruins of Buddhist places of worship in the form of pillars, gateways, statues of Buddha, etc., near the erstwhile site of the Keshav Dev temple in Mathura. Other excavations in and around Mathura, uncovered statues (now displayed in Mathura Museum) that had a Greek design, including a few that had inscriptions of the Indo-Greek Kushan king Kanishka who established Buddhism as the state religion in the 1st century CE. Some of these were found while the foundation of the new residence of the District Collector of Mathura was being dug soon after the 1857 War of Independence.

Archaeological evidence from the excavation of the Jaini Tila or Kankali mound (off the Mathura–Vrindavan road, near the present-day Bhuteshwar temple) reveals that Jainism (a religion older than Buddhism) also thrived in Mathura

The Kankali Mound today

from 2nd century BCE to the 12th century CE, i.e. for a continuous period of 1400 years. Many of these articles were enormous in dimension, and remarkably well preserved. They can be seen in the exquisitely designed Government Jain Museum in the city. This is not to say that Mathura was ever a predominantly Jain city but that Jainism (and Hinduism) coexisted within a predominant Buddhist environment for a long period of Mathura's history. The significance of the archaeological discoveries is that they provide concrete proof of Mathura as an ancient city, which is at least 2500 years old.

The revival of Hinduism in all of India, which began during the Guptas and vigorously continued under Harsha Vardhan (606–647 CE), meant that by the time the Arabs and Mahmud of Ghazni invaded India (712 CE and 1000 CE respectively), Mathura had reverted to be a Hindu city, and indeed a very wealthy one. Between 1000 and 1027 CE, Mahmud of Ghazni invaded India 17 times and it was in his ninth invasion in 1017 that he sacked the city of Mathura. According to the account *Tarikh-i-Yamini* written by his own secretary Abu Al Utbi, Mahmud's army plundered the city for 20 days, carrying away more than 100 camel-loads of gold idols, precious stones and silver images. Prosperity gradually returned to Mathura but then it was sacked again for religious reasons by Sikandar Lodi, an overzealous Muslim ruler of the Delhi Sultanate (1489–1517 CE).

Fortunately for the next 150 years or so, Mathura benefitted from benevolent Muslim rule. Under Sher Shah Suri, the 'Sadak-e-Azam' (later, the Grand Trunk Road) that passes through the length of Mathura district, was

Conch blower statue made from red sandstone (1st/2nd CE) found in an excavation at Mathura

Residence of District Collector, Mathura

vastly improved and a number of *serai*s or rest houses were constructed en route. The Mughal emperor Akbar is said to have paid a friendly visit to Swami Haridas, the music teacher of Tansen (one of his *nav ratna*s), at Nidhi Van in Vrindavan. This was also the time when the saints of the Bhakti Movement Vallabhacharya (1486–1531 CE) and Chaitanya Mahaprabhu (1489–1534 CE) visited Mathura with their message of Lord Krishna. Indeed, the worship of Lord Krishna as practised today in the Braj region, including the *parikrama*, the Ras Leela and other rituals, originated in the teachings of these two saints and their immediate disciples.

Then followed a period of temple building devoted to the Krishna legend, culminating in the Keshav Dev Temple, constructed around 1620 in Mathura by Vir Singh Bundela, the Raja of Orchha. Built at a cost of Rs 33 lakhs, it was described by the French traveller Tavernier in 1650 as being of vast size, visible from a distance of 5–6 kos (9–10 miles).

In February 1669, however, Aurangzeb personally descended on Mathura and destroyed the temple, carrying away the idols, all adorned with costly jewels, to Agra. Shortly thereafter, the Shahi Idgah mosque was built on the site of the temple and Aurangzeb changed the name of Mathura to Islamabad and Vrindavan to Mominabad. For the next 150 years or so, Mathura became a fairly desolate city. It remained, nonetheless, a place of pilgrimage for Hindus with Brahmin priests performing rituals at a few selected temples in Mathura and Vrindavan. The decline of Mughal power following the death of Aurangzeb, meant that for brief periods, Mathura came under the tutelage of local Jat rulers of Bharatpur as well as Marathas who ruled from Agra. During this period too, Mathura was sacked once again, this time by the Afghan invader Ahmed Shah Abdali who, while retreating from the forces of Surajmal, the Jat ruler of Bharatpur, in 1757, looted the city and massacred over a thousand of its citizens.

The British took over the administration of Mathura in 1803 after defeating the Scindia army in a battle at Agra. All public lands, roads etc. were transferred from the control of the local Maratha governor to the government of British India. Initially the administrative headquarters were at Sadabad, a nearby town, but in 1832, Mathura was made the headquarters of a district with the same name, part of Agra Division of the North West Provinces (later rearranged as the United Provinces of Agra and Oudh, and then the United Provinces). A military cantonment came to be established along the banks of the Yamuna in 1810. Four gates were constructed at the entrance points of Mathura city called Bharatpur, Deegh, Vrindavan and Holi Gates, indicating the destination of the exits, the last one being the exit towards Agra.

The restoration of religious freedom under British rule led to the building of some of Mathura's most revered temples, beginning with the Dwarkadheesh temple (Mathura, 1813), the Rangji Temple (Vrindavan, 1851) and the Bankey Bihari Temple (Vrindavan, 1864). The British also introduced the railways to the city via rail link to Hathras (1875) and the Mathura–Vrindavan link (1889); Mathura Junction on the main line came up in 1904. The Agra Canal brought water from the Yamuna barrage in Delhi to the parched lands of Mathura district in 1874; the Mathura Museum was set up in 1874 to house its precious archaeological finds.

Post-Independence, Mathura, now a district in the state of Uttar Pradesh, emerged as a place of national importance. Due to its strategic location near the nation's capital, important units of the Indian army have been stationed at the Mathura Cantonment. Commissioned in 1983, then North India's largest oil refinery came up in Mathura to cater to the demand of petroleum products in North West part of the country and the National Capital Region. The erstwhile UP College of Veterinary Science and Animal Husbandry, Uttar Pradesh's first veterinary college and the fourth in the country was set up in Mathura in 1947, an appropriate location, given the importance of the cow in Hindu rituals. The opening of the Yamuna Expressway linking Delhi to Agra in 2012

shortened the travel time to Vrindavan and Mathura, which has increased the flow of pilgrims exponentially.

The task of reconstructing the Keshav Dev Temple began in the 1950s and was completed by 1982. It is now known as the Krishna Janam Bhumi Temple. In fact, after Independence, there has been a flurry of construction of new shrines, each more impressive than the other. Today, with its beautiful temples, festivals, *parikramas*, holy men and cow shelters, Mathura, the sacred land of the Hindus from time immemorial, remains an iconic pilgrimage destination of India.

Built in 1874, the Holi Gate on the traditional Agra road remains the epicentre of activities in the old city.

Legend of Sri Krishna

In the Bhagavad Gita, Hinduism's holiest book, God himself states that He would manifest himself in the world to restore order whenever the world faced a rise in evil and chaos and decline in righteousness:

Yada yada hi dharmasya glanirbhavati bharata,
Abhythanamadharmasya tadatmanam srijamyaham,
Paritranaya sadhunang vinashay cha dushkritam,
Dharmasangsthapanarthay sambhavami yuge yuge.

Bhagavad Gita (Chapter 4, verses 7–8)

Going by mythology, it so happened that a long time ago, Mathura was ruled by Kansa, a wicked and exceedingly cruel king. The people of Mathura prayed to God to rescue them from this evil ruler. When his atrocities continued unabated, God decided to descend to earth and sent a warning message to Kansa that his destroyer would take birth as the eighth son of Vasudev and Devaki who hailed from Govardhan. Upon

Miniature painting depicting Vasudev crossing the Yamuna with the infant Krishna Source: National Archives, New Delhi

hearing this message, Kansa summoned the two to Mathura and kept a close eye on the couple. He then embarked upon the diabolical act of murdering every male child born to Devaki. Once she became pregnant for the eighth time, Kansa ordered Devaki imprisoned in Mathura jail. On the night God took birth in the incarnation of Krishna, all prison guards fell into a stupor by His will, and father Vasudev was able to smuggle the child out. Baby Krishna was then exchanged for a girl child born to Nand and Yashoda in Gokul, situated on the opposite bank of the Yamuna, who replaced him in the prison cell. Kansa was thus fooled to believe that Devaki had given birth to a daughter.

Krishna was thereafter brought up in secrecy under the love and care of his foster parents, Nand and Yashoda, along with his older sibling, Balram. This was the time when he began performing his well-known miracles. The wicked demoness Pootna who had become suspicious, tried to breastfeed poisonous milk to baby Krishna, but was destroyed by him. As he grew, Krishna roamed the meadows and forests of the Braj region with his herds of cattle. A favorite pastime of his was playing the flute and frolicking with the local milkmaids, fairest among whom was Radha who became the consort of the adolescent Krishna. Other miracles continued to happen. The gigantic river serpent Kaliya who had been harassing innocent people who came down to the Yamuna was eliminated by Krishna. He also saved the citizens of Govardhan from the wrath of the displeased rain god Indra by lifting the Giriraj Mountain on his little finger as a protective shield from the storm unleashed upon them.

Finally, the evil king Kansa was killed by Krishna by hurling him into a crevice after a brief battle. Peace returned

Tableau at Prem Mandir, Vrindavan depicting Krishna lifting the Govardhan mountain

once more to Braj. His job done, Krishna departed for Dwarka (in present-day Gujarat) where he ruled for many years in glory. He married Rukmani, joined hands with the Pandava brothers in their battle against the evil Duryodhan, as told in the Mahabharata, and performed many other brave deeds. Though he never returned, his legend lives on in Mathura, in its temples and festivals, its arts and crafts, its songs and dances and in the everyday lives of its people.

Krishna Lore in Indian Art

Indian art is a syncretic expression of the rich heritage of an ancient culture, religion and mythology. Of all the gods that are associated with the arts in India, Krishna has been the most popular. The Krishna lore pervades the visual and performing arts in all of India. Be it the miniature paintings of Basohli or Kangra in the north, or Tanjore paintings of the south, the Nathdwara Pichhwai paintings in the west, or the Manuscript paintings of Assam in the east, the inspiration was drawn from the Puranas and Jayadeva's *Geet Govind* which tell the story of Krishna. Following the Bhakti movement, almost all forms of artistic expression became a means to serve the Lord. Music, dance, painting, sculpture, embroidery, theatre, poetry and cuisine, were directed towards telling the story of, or propitiating Lord Krishna, who was master for some, the naughty, but dear child for some, and the friend or lover for others. Both folk and classical Indian art are immensely inspired by the charming god, Krishna, who endeared Himself to all, by His *leela*s (miracles).

Pichhwai street souvenir of Krishna's Ras Leela with gopies

The Guruvayur Temple in Kerala, stands out as a Krishna temple, where the Geet Govind is sung and danced to, and Narayana Bhattathiri's 16th century poem on Krishna "Narayaneeyam" is still recited in its precincts. The Krishnattam dance, using Sanskrit lyrics, is a regular feature there. The Padmanabhaswamy Temple in Kerala resounds with Swathi Thirunal's compositions addressed to Lord Krishna. The Alvar poets of the first millennium sang in Tamil of Krishna. The classical Kannada song "Krishna Ni Begani Baro…" made

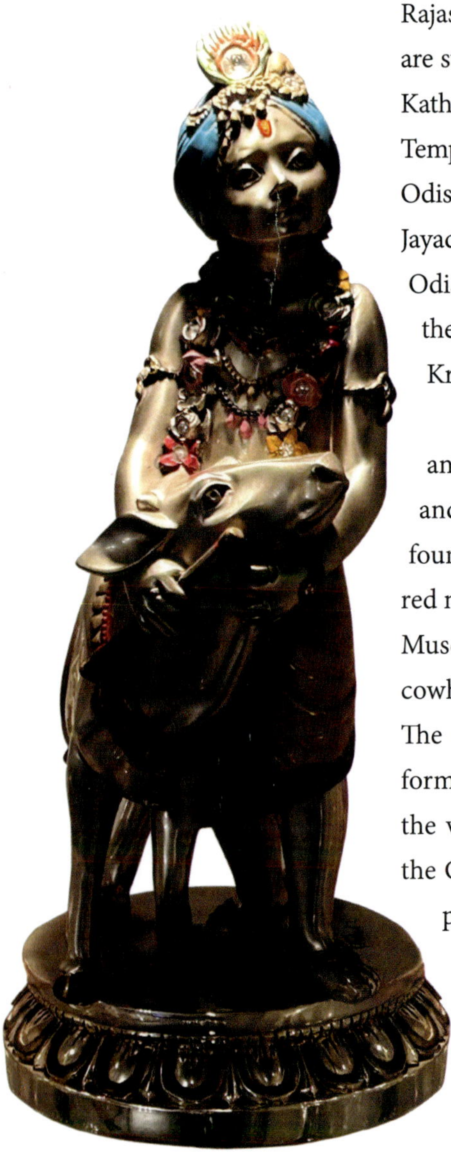

famous by the danseuse Bala Saraswati, by her Bharatnatyam performance was composed in the Srikrishna Temple at Udupi.

In the west of India, Narsinh Mehta of Gujarat and Mirabai of Rajasthan, composed memorable devotional songs of Krishna, that are still sung and appreciated by music lovers. Haveli Sangeet and Kathak have a long association with Rajasthan and the Srinathji Temple at Nathdwara. In the east, the Jagannath Temple at Puri, Odisha, has maintained an unbroken tradition of the rendition of Jayadeva's "Ashtapadis" (eight-line verses) every night, to authentic Odissi *raga*s and *tala*s. The Govinda Temple in Imphal is home to the Manipuri dance that celebrates the divine love of Radha and Krishna in the form of the Rasa dances.

The first stone sculptures of Krishna and his father Vasudeva and Samkarshana (another name of his elder brother, Balram) and Ekanamsa (another name for his sister, Yogmaya), were found in the archaeological excavations at Mathura. Carved in red mottled sandstone, these statues can be seen in the Mathura Museum. In the Gupta period, the aspect of Krishna Gopala, the cowherd, became popular in Mathura, Rajasthan and the south. The southern Indian bronze statues of Krishna in His various forms—Venugopal, the divine flute player; Kaliya Mardana, the vanquisher of the snake Kaliya; Gopala, the cowherd; and the Chola bronze of baby Krishna with butter-ball in hand, are popular gifting objects. Wooden statues of Andhra Pradesh and stone carvings of Tamil Nadu celebrating Krishna are popular handicrafts. Marble statues of the God made in Rajasthan and other places are found in temples and homes. The 18th-century Bishnupur temples of Bengal are famous for their terracotta sculptures of Krishna.

Miniature paintings in North India began as illustrations for text in religious manuscripts. Bilhana's *Chaura-Panchaskita*, in the thirteenth century, and the fifteenth century versions of Jayadeva's *Geet Govind* and Swami Bilwamangala's *Balagopal Stuti* are richly illustrated in this manner. Notable miniature paintings inspired by the Krishna lore, are those from Mewar, Kota and Kishangarh in Rajasthan, Malwa and Bundelkhand in central India and Pahari miniatures from Basohli and Kangra.

Apart from these, indigenous art from Mithila (Bihar), Kalighat (Bengal), Paithani (Maharashtra), Kalamkari (Andhra Pradesh), Pichhwai (Rajasthan and Mathura) represent the best of Indian folk art. The styles of Kanhai of Vrindavan, and Raja Ravi Verma have been trend-setting in Indian painting. In recent times, Anjolie Ela Menon's Murano glass creations of Bala Gopala have also reached iconic status.

Jayadeva's classic poem on Krishna and Radha, *Geet Govind*, has been set to *ragas* and *talas*, and adapted to a variety of singing styles ranging from the Hindustani classical styles of the Gwalior and Benares Gharanas, the Kirtan style of Bengal, Manipur and Odisha, the Carnatic style in Tamil Nadu, the Sopanam style in Kerala temples, and the Bhajan tradition accompanied by the Kummi dance in Karnataka.

Krishna *leela*s and *Raas Leela*s are performed in temples and theatres across India, around the festivals of Janamashtami and Holi. In modern times, Hindi films and television, have carried forward the Krishna theme. Peter Brook's *Mahabharata* stormed the international theatre and film world in the late 1980s, proving that Krishna's appeal is universal.

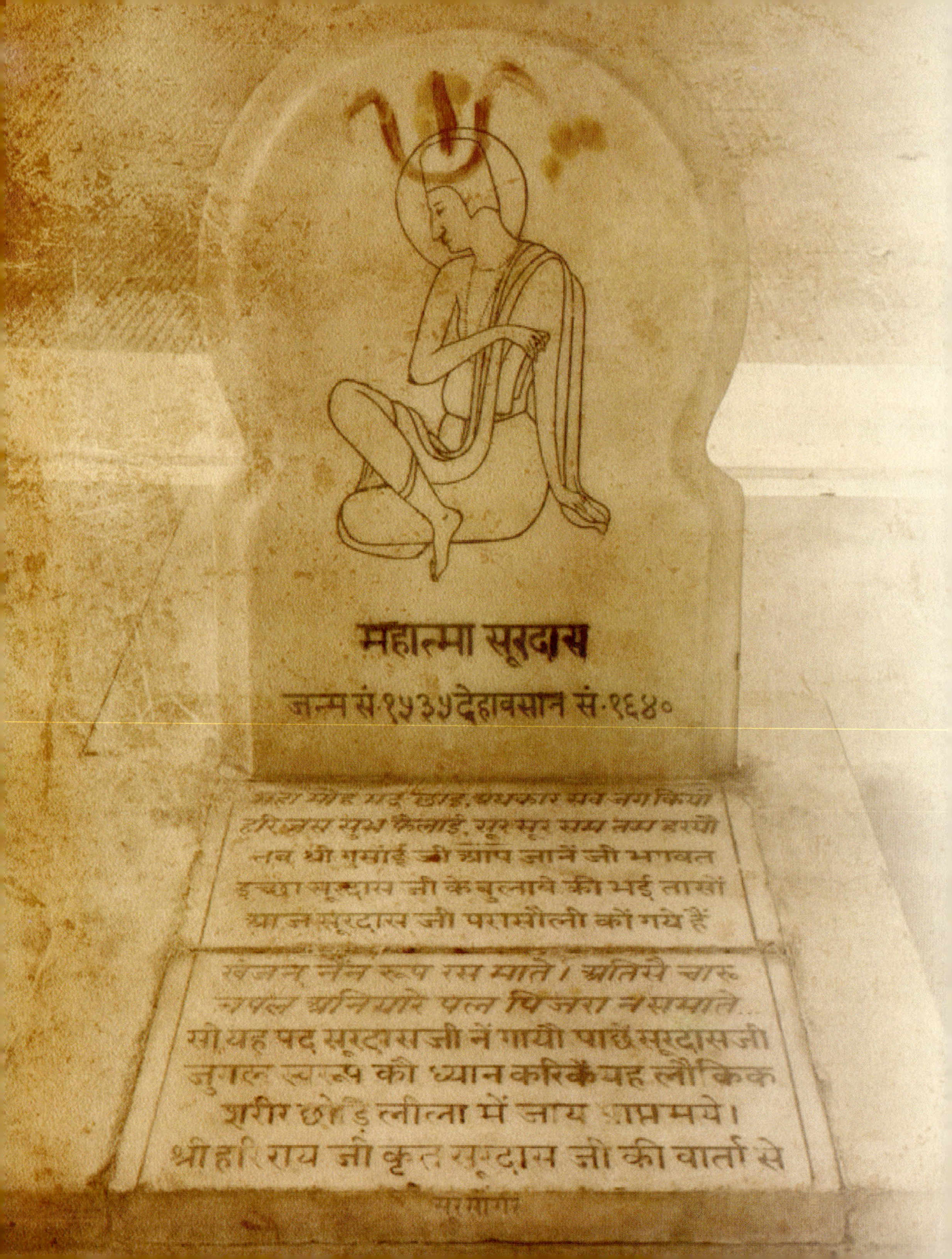
महात्मा सूरदास
जन्म सं॰ १५३५ देहावसान सं॰ १६४०
तब श्री गुसांई जी आप जानें जो भगवत
इच्छा सूरदास जी के बुलाने की भई तातें
आज सूरदास जी परासौली कों गये हैं
खंजन नैन रूप रस माते। अतिसै चारु
चपल अनियारे पल पिंजरा न समाते...
सो यह पद सूरदासजी नें गायौ पाछें सूरदासजी
जुगल स्वरूप कौ ध्यान करिकैं यह लौकिक
शरीर छोड़ लीला में जाय प्राप्त भये।
श्री हरिराय जी कृत सूरदास जी की वार्ता से

Braj Bhasha

No book on Mathura can be complete without reference to Braj Bhasha, the language of the region. A dialect of Hindi, it was, along with Awadhi, the main language of Hindi literature before Hindustani became popular in the 19th century. Much of the Hindi poetry taught to high school students in India is in Braj Bhasha even today. The focus in North Indian classical vocal music might be on the notes of the *raga*, but the lyrics are mostly in Braj Bhasha.

Braj Bhasha is widely spoken in the villages of central and western Uttar Pradesh, including Mathura, Agra, Aligarh, Mainpuri; Bharatpur in extreme Eastern Rajasthan; Dholpur in the northern tip of Madhya Pradesh and in Southern Haryana. Among its users was Amir Khusro (1253–1325 CE) the musician, poet and scholar, who was born in Patiali, Kasganj, a district adjacent to Mathura. His Sufi composition "*Chhaap tilak sab chheeni, mosey naina milayi ke*" ('You have taken away my looks, my identity, by just a glance') in Braj Bhasha continues to be popular till this day. The saint-poet Tulsidas (1532–1623 CE), author of *Ramcharitmanas*,

Tomb of the 17th century Braj Bhasha poet Raskhan, restored by Braj Teerth Vikas Parishad

wrote his *Vinay Patrika* in the same language. Surdas, the blind poet (1478–1583 CE), who lived in village Parsoli near Govardhan, was perhaps, the biggest exponent of Braj Bhasha. His collection *Sursagar* is full of odes towards the infant Lord Krishna, like the all-time favourite *bhajan* (devotional song) *"Maiyya mori main nahin makhan khayo"* ('Mother mine, I never ate the butter'). Braj Bhasha was also the language of Harivansh, a medieval saint of Vrindavan and author of *Chaurasi Pad*, 84 poems on the love between Krishna and Radha. Other famous poets who wrote in the language were Bihari, Raskhan, Taj Bibi and Rahim as well as the Ashth Chhaap (club of eight) poet-followers of Vallabhacharya.

The language is close to Hindi but there are important differences. Often the *a* sound is substituted by *o* as in *chalo gayo* instead of *chala gaya* ('gone away'). The substitution is also done in reverse as in *Wa* instead of *Woh* ('he/she'). A few common words/sentences in the language are given below which the visitor to Braj might find useful while interacting with locals, especially in the satellite towns and villages of Mathura district.

English	Hindi	Braj Bhasha
Hello	Namaste	Radhe Radhe
I dont understand	Main nahin samjha	Main nai samajhyo
What's his name?	Uska kya naam hai?	Wako ka naam hay?
Yes	Haan	Humbay
No	Nahin	Nai
Please	Kripaya	Kripa Karau
Boy/Girl	Ladka/Ladki	Lalla/Lali
I don't know	Mujhe nahin pata	Moi nai patau
How long will it take?	Kitna samay lagega?	Kitek samay lagego?
Thanks!	Dhanyavad	Jai ho tihari!

Some representative Braj bhasha poetry:

मैया मोरी मैं नहीं माखन खायो !
भोर भयो गैयन के पाछे
तूने मोहे मधुबन पठायो
चार पहर बंछी वट भटक्यों, साँझ परे घर आयो।
मैं कब माखन खायो ?

Mother mine, I never ate the butter!
At dawn you sent me out with the cows
I spent all day grazing them in the forest while playing my flute,

and returned home only in the evening,
When could I have eaten the butter?

—*Sursagar* by Surdas (1478–1583)

छाप तिलक सब छिनी
मोसे नैना मिलाइके
प्रेमभटी का मदवा पिलाइके
मतवाली कर लीनी
मोसे नैना मिलाइके

You have stolen my name, my identity,
With just a glance
Making me drink the nectar of love,
You have got me intoxicated
With just a glance.

—Amir Khusro (1253–1325)

सुनो मेरो वचन छबिली राधा
ते पायो रस सिंधु अमादा
तेरो रूप कहत नहीं आवे
हित हरिवंश कछूक जस गावे

Hear me, O graceful Radha
You have found an ocean of joy
Your beauty cannot be described in words
Hit Harivansh can sing only a little of your glory

—*Chaurasi Pad* by Hit Harivansh (1473–1552)

मानुस हौं तो वही रसखान, बसों मिली गोकुल गांव के गंवारन
जो पसु हौं तो कहा बस मेरो, चरों नित नंद की धेनु मँझारन
पाहन हौं तो वही गिरी को, जो धरो कर छत्र पुरंदर धारन
जो खग हौं तो बसेरो करौं मिली कालिंदी-कूल-कदंब की डारन

In my next life, if I am reborn as Raskhan,
I shall again reside with the milkmaids of Gokul,
If reborn as an animal, I would like to be born as Krishna's cow,
If reborn as a stone, I should be part of the mountain lifted
by Krishna with his little finger,
If reborn as a raven, I shall live on a branch of
the Kadamb tree on the Yamuna bank

—Raskhan (1548–1628)

छैल जो छबीला, सब रंग का रंगीला,
बड़ा चित्त का अड़ीला, कहूं देवता से न्यारा है,
नंदजू का प्यारा, जिन कंस को पछारा,
वह वृंदावन वारा, कृष्ण साहब हमारा है

Krishna, the resident of Vrindavan
Is naughty, colourful and unique among all the gods,
He is the beloved son of Nand, who vanquished Kansa,
But he is tender of heart, and is the Lord of my life

—Taj Bibi

A Kaleidoscope of Culture and Art

Divinity has inspired art from time immemorial, not only in India, but in cultures all over the world. The story of Krishna, and the fact that he was born in Mathura and blessed the soil, hills, forests, groves, ponds and the river Yamuna with his presence, is alive even to this day. Popular belief establishes Mathura (in Braj) and Dwarka (in present-day Gujarat) as Lord Krishna's birthplace and kingdom respectively.

The earliest recorded archaeological finds from Mathura, are the red sandstone sculptures of Buddha, Bodhisattvas and Yakshas, dating back to the 2nd century BCE. Towering figures of the Jain Tirthankars, in yellow and red sandstone, can be seen in the Jain Museum, close to the Mathura Collectorate. The main Government Mathura Museum is a treasure trove of both Kushana (2–/3rd century BCE–3rd century CE) and Gupta (c. 4th–7th centuries CE) era sculptures. After this time, most of the sculptures were of Hindu gods and goddesses. According to historians, Mathura was the first centre of art to produce devotional icons for all the three faiths, namely, Buddhism, Jainism and

above: *Unique Gupta period sculpture of Cosmic Vishnu, excavated from Keshav Dev Temple premises*
facing page: *Yakshis trampling evil forces, Bhuteswar, Mathura, 2nd century CE (Indian Museum, Kolkata)*

Hinduism. The Mathura School of Sculpture was distinct from the Gandhara School of Art. The latter was influenced by the Greco-Roman styles of sculpture, whereas, the Mathura school drew inspiration from the regional styles of sculptures, like the Yaksha sculptures, which are believed to be male fertility spirits.

The human-like depiction of various deities, apparently, started to appear in the middle of the 1st century BCE. Panini, a Sanskrit philologist, grammarian, scholar and the author of *Ashtadhyayi,* and Patanjali, mystic and philosopher, and the author of many Sanskrit works

facing page above:
3rd century CE double-faced Shivling, at Mathura Museum

facing page below:
Sculpture of Kartikey with spear, 1st century CE, at Mathura Museum

below:
2nd century sculpture of Vasudev crossing the Yamuna under the protection of the serpent Shesh Nag, at Mathura Museum

including the *Yoga Sutras*, seem to mention depictions of Shiva, Skanda, Visaka, Vasudeva-Krishna and Arjuna. In particular, the worship of Balram-Samkarshana and Vasudeva-Krishna, seems to have originated in Mathura, where they were revered as members of the five 'Vrishni' (an ancient Vedic Indian clan) heroes.

The revival of the Vaishnav sect and the Bhakti movement in the 16th century brought about a cultural and artistic renaissance in Mathura–Vrindavan. The two leading luminaries of the Bhakti movement, Chaitanya Mahaprabhu and Sri Vallabhacharya, set the ritualistic narrative for the devotees which continues to the present day. Every art form was employed to please the Lord. Music, dance, painting, floral art, cooking, stitching and embroidery, metalcraft, woodcraft and other such art forms, are part of the temple tradition of Mathura and Vrindavan, and are offered as 'Seva', or service, to the deities. A few examples of these arts are, namely, Sanjhi, Pichhwai, Kanhai paintings, Phool Bangla, Charkula dance, Mayur dance, Raas.

Sanjhi

Sanjhi, is derived from the word *sanjh*, which means dusk. It is believed to be an ancient art, prevalent in the *Dwapar Yug*, or the age of Krishna, and also finds mention in the Vedas. It is said that Radha and the *gopi*s would make colourful patterns with flower petals or powdered colours on the ground, waiting for Krishna to return with the cows, at dusk.

This art has been preserved in the temples of Mathura and Vrindavan over the centuries. Traditionally, priests or artists make Sanjhi during the period of *Pitr Paksh* corresponding with the month of October, when ancestors are remembered. There are many different ways of making Sanjhi. There is the dry colour Sanjhi, on a hard surface, *Jal Sanjhi*, done under water or over water in a *thali* (platter), Sanjhi made with flowers and Sanjhi made with cow dung.

Dry colour Sanjhi

The theme, invariably, is Radha-Krishna. The making of Sanjhi is done discreetly, behind curtains, as it is considered a sacred exercise. The making of a Sanjhi is a tedious process of sprinkling dry colours over paper stencils. The making of paper stencils is an art by itself. In the old days, the stencils were made of thin silver sheets, with patterns embossed and then cut out. The art has evolved over time, and paper has replaced silver, and scissors have given way to sharp pen-knives. The making of dry colour Sanjhi involves preparing the surface, placing the stencil on it and sifting dry colours, overlapping colour after colour to produce the final image, a process which takes four to five hours. In the evening, at sunset, the Sanjhi is unveiled to the devotees to the singing of Sanjhi *pada*s. It is a magical experience.

Dry colour Sanjhi with lush detailing

In recent years, the Braj Foundation has restored the Brahm Kund (sacred tank) at Vrindavan, which was, in ancient times, the site for an annual Sanjhi fair, and organises a festival to celebrate this ancient art form.

right:
Jal Sanjhi in a thali

below:
Floral Sanjhi

Pichhwai

Pichhwai paintings originated in Nathdwara, Rajasthan, in the 17th century, and reached Mathura–Vrindavan, along with the priests, artists and devotees of the Pushti Marg sect of Krishna worshipers. There are a handful of Pichhwai artists in Vrindavan, who paint in this tradition. Pichhwais are backdrops for the deity in the sanctum sanctorum. They are paintings on cloth.

Originally, vegetable colours were used, but now, chemical colours have become popular owing to the ease of availability and the wide range of hues on offer. Sometimes, gold leaves are used as embellishment. The paintings depict pastimes or *Leela*s of Krishna, festivals such as Janamashtami, Sharad Poornima, Annakoot, Gopashtami, Daan Leela and Raas Leela. Some paintings have icons of Yamuna and Vallabhacharya. The Pichhwais draw inspiration from the *Bhagwat Purana*. These works of art, apart from their artistic appeal, are a means to evoke the *Bhakti Ras*, or devotion for Sri Krishna, and also to narrate the tales of Sri Krishna to the masses.

Pichhwai as temple backdrop

In some temples, the Pichhwais are changed eight times a day (the eight *prahar*), and also according to the festival calendar, or seasons, to provide an appropriate ambience to please the Lord. The summer Pichhwais have water bodies and lotus flowers, to provide a cooling effect, whereas, in winter, warm colours such as red and gold are used on the paintings. In some temples of Vrindavan, during the period of Holi, the backdrop behind the deity is white, and wet or dry colours are splashed or thrown on them, to the singing of Holi songs. In other temples, it is done artistically, till a colourful pattern emerges.

Over time, Pichhwai paintings have become sought-after collectibles, and also inspire fashion designers, architects and interior decorators, finding their way to boutiques, homes and commercial spaces and art-galleries.

Pichwai as temple backdrop

Krishna Couture

The religious economy of Mathura is largely centered around the three types of *seva* (service) offered to the deities, namely, *bhog* (food offering), *raag* (music in the form of *bhajan, kirtan*), and *shringar* (adornment).

Shringar involves a number of things such as the decorations, Pichhwais, rituals of bathing and dressing-up the *vigraha*s (idols), their jewellery and accessories. The *poshak* (clothes), *mukut* (crown) and jewellery for the deities, made in Mathura and Vrindavan, are a cottage industry. Several homes, particularly, in the Gaura Nagar area, are engaged in stitching and embroidery of *poshak*, from the tiniest to life-size ones. Dress-material of all kinds, silk, cotton, satin and taffeta, are used, with trimmings and appliqué, silk-thread embroidery and Zardozi (gold thread embroidery), bead and mirror work etc. Each artisan and couturier strives to produce the best *poshak* for the *vigraha*s. The *poshak* changes from season to season, and also according to the time of the day. For instance, light cotton clothes are for the summer; night-wear, woollen and silk ones for winter; yellow for Janamashtami, green for *Savan* (the rainy month), and so on.

The costumes are also varied, small frock-like dresses for 'Laddoo-Gopal' (infant Krishna), *dhoti* and *angavastra* for the bigger *vigraha*s. Accessories such as crowns, turbans, turban inserts, necklaces,

Adornments for the infant Krishna

armlets, anklets, waistbands, *tulsi*-bead necklaces etc., are used as adornments. *Lehengas* (long skirts), for the female deities, *chunris* and jewellery for them are also made here. An estimated 20,000 men and women produce beautiful costumes and jewellery that find their way to temples and homes in Mathura, rest of India and abroad.

Kanhai Paintings

The Kanhai School of Art, founded by the award winning Kanhai Chitrakar (1934–2013) is Vrindavan's own style of painting. Kanhai paintings, though relatively recent in origin, draw inspiration from the Tanjore and Nathdwara Schools of painting. Kanhai paintings follow a distinct style. The subject is Krishna, along with Radha and the *gopis*. The paintings are mostly portraits embellished with gold leaf and crystals. The paintings are oil on canvas. Facial expressions and proportionate representation of the facial and body features, set them apart from the Tanjore and Nathdwara styles of painting.

Over time this art is evolving and becoming more contemporary, while being rooted in tradition, but being open to new ideas. The Kanhai Art Gallery at Vrindavan is a preferred stop for art lovers.

Oil on canvas paintings of the Kanhai School, Vrindavan

Phool Bangla

Ay dou baithey ri, kusum Kunj bhawan
vividh rang puhupani ke bhushan, pila saajat pyari ju tan.

'The (divine) couple sits in the house of flowers
adorned with floral jewellery of a myriad colours,
and the yellow colour stands out on Radha ji.'

—Swami Haridas

Phool Bangla is a tribute to Sri Krishna's love for nature. Literally, it means a house of flowers. It is a temple tradition of Vrindavan and Mathura. It is said that Sri Krishna loved to be around tree groves and flowers, and was adept at the art of making garlands and decorating with flowers, one of the 64 *kalas* (arts) mastered by Him at Guru Sandeepan's ashram. Reference to Phool Bangla by other names such as *Kusum Kunj*, *Phool Mahal* and *Phool Baithak*, is found in old manuscripts of the 16th, 17th and 18th centuries. The *Srimad Bhagwat*, *Padma Purana*, *Sursagar* (by Surdas) and

Hit Chaurasi (by Sri Hit Harivansh Goswami), mention Phool Bangla as a form of *seva*.

The Bhakti tradition visualises Sri Krishna as a divine form, while at the same time attributing all human feelings and emotions to Him, as a way to form a close connection with the divine. The changing seasons, then, call for different kinds of *seva* to the Lord. The *vigrah* in the temples are shielded from the scorching summer heat by constructing Phool Bangla. The flowers provide a cool and fragrant ambience to the gods. The deity is taken out of the sanctum sanctorum and placed in the Phool Bangla, and for the devotees, it is a special occasion for *darshan*. The Phool Bangla at the Bankey Bihari Temple in Vrindavan is unique in its beauty, and it is the only time in the year when the divine feet of the deities can be seen. The other prominent temples where this tradition is still followed are Sri Radha Raman Temple, Sri Radha Vallabh Temple, Seva Kunj, Shah Ji Temple and Sri Ranganath Temple. The making of the Phool Bangla is sponsored by devotees, and offered as *seva* to the deities.

The Phool Bangla is usually a three-tiered structure, consisting of *thaath* (frames or panels) made of bamboo or wood, held together with nails. Strings of flowers of jasmine, rose, tuberose and marigold, and leaves of the Ashoka tree are pegged on the frame to form a lattice design. Colourful highlights are created by arrangements of gladioli, gerbera and orchids. Plantain stems are cut in strips to cover the frame, and the pith is cut in various shapes to create floral, bird or animal shapes. The panels have a designated place in the structure, the deity is placed centre-stage. In addition,

Phool Bangla being set up in Bankey Bihari Temple, Vrindavan

jhaad, or chandeliers of flowers, are suspended from the temple ceiling, enhancing the look of the Phool Bangla. The making of the Phool Bangla is a labour intensive and time-consuming process, commencing in the morning, reaching completion towards late afternoon, in time for the evening *darshan*.

Visitors or pilgrims who want to see this beautiful ancient art, should plan to visit anytime between *Kamada Ekadashi* and *Hariyali Amavasya*, that is, the months of *Vaishakh*, *Jyeshtha* and *Ashadh*, according to the Hindu calendar. By the Gregorian calendar, it would coincide with early April to mid-July, a period of 100 days.

Charkula Dance

If there is one dance which can be said to belong to Mathura, it is the Charkula dance, which is said to have originated in the village of Mukhrai, named after Mukhra Devi, the grandmother of Radha Rani. Associated with the legend of Radha-Krishna, it is traditionally performed on the third day of the Holi festivities, when Radha was born. But in recent times, it is performed at the end of the Holi festivities at some places, or at various auspicious occasions, and cultural or corporate events.

The local legend is that when infant Radha was born, her maternal grandmother, Mukhra Devi, to announce the happy news, lit earthen lamps, placed them on a chariot wheel, balanced it on her head, and danced with joy. Even to this day, most Charkula dancers come from the Mukhrai village, a short distance from Mathura. Another story is that

facing page:
Charkula dancers

it is reminiscent of the lifting of the Govardhan hill by Sri Krishna, and celebrates His victory over Indra, the Rain God.

The dance has evolved over time. In its present form, women in long skirts and colourful blouses, with veils covering their faces, balance a five-tiered circular wooden pyramid (Charkula) on their heads, with 108 lit oil lamps placed on them. They dance gracefully, to the beat of drums and cymbals, and the singing of 'Rasiya' songs (devotional folk songs of Braj). The movements are slow and restricted as they balance the Charkula weighing around 50 kg. Their footwork, synchronised to the beat of the music, their arms, moving in wavy motions, and the light of the oil lamps and the colourful costumes, render a mesmerising sight.

The piety of the dancer and the devotees at a celebration

Mayur Dance

This is a popular folk dance of the Braj region. The dance depicts an episode from the story of Radha and Krishna. It is said that one day Radha was at Mor Kuti, a place near Gehravar Vana at Barsana, and was longing to see her beloved Krishna, while watching peacocks dance. Then, to her surprise, Krishna appeared in the guise of a peacock and danced for Radha. This divine *leela* is performed to this day by dance troupes on various occasions. The colourful costumes and peacock plumage are very attractive, and the dance movements imitating the peacocks are very enchanting.

Raas Leela

The *Bhagwat Purana* mentions the Raas Leela as a divine pastime of Sri Krishna with Radha and the *gopi*s. It is often referred to as the dance of divine love. On a higher plane, it symbolises the oneness with the divine, and cosmic harmony.

According to the Bhagwat, the Raas was performed on full-moon nights, when Krishna played the flute, and the *gopi*s would join Him, entranced. The Maha Raas (Great Raas) was on the night of *Sharad Poornima* (autumnal full-moon), when multiple Krishnas danced with *gopi*s.

Raas Leela performance was started by Swami Sri Uddhavaghamanda Devacharya in the early 15th century at Bansivat in Vrindavan, Mathura. It was popularised in the 17th and 18th century, by Sri Vallabhacharya and Sri Vitthalanatha. Vrindavan's Raas Leela is considered a

forerunner of Kathak. It celebrates the life and tales of Krishna from his childhood till his adolescence.

The climax of a Maha Raas performance

This living theatre is performed by dance troupes called the Raasdhari Mandalis, who go from place to place performing. The person playing the role of Krishna is considered a *swaroop* (incarnation) of the Lord, and worshipped as one during the performance. In the old days, the dancers were only boys, but now girls play the part of Radha and the *gopi*s, and a male dancer plays the part of Sri Krishna. Sometimes, only girls perform all characters. This art form is a visual treat. The beautiful costumes in different hues, and the choreography in the Kathak style of dance, create an enchanting atmosphere for the audience. This folk dance is performed on Janmashtami, but lately, the dance troupes are busy all year round, performing at various events and celebrations.

Brajbhoomi

Rajadhani tatah sabhut
sarva-yadava-bhu-bhujam
Mathura bhagavan yatra
nityam sannihito harih

(The city of Mathura has been the capital of all the kings of the Yadu dynasty. The city and district of Mathura are very intimately connected with Krishna, for Lord Krishna lives there eternally.)

Bhagwat Purana (10.1.28)

The city of Mathura straddles the area between the Delhi–Agra Highway (NH 44) on the west and the Yamuna River on the east. On its eastern parts lies the old city with its numerous *ghats* (river bathing sites), the civil lines and the military cantonment. The western part is more recent and is home to a number of new educational institutions. The cantonment houses elite regiments of the Indian army, besides UP's oldest veterinary university. The large Mathura oil refinery lies a short distance away on the south-western outskirts of the city. Notwithstanding its modern growth trajectory, Mathura remains best known for its historic and religious sites, as one of Hinduism's seven sacred cities (besides Ayodhya, Haridwar, Varanasi, Kanchipuram, Ujjain and Dwarka, as mentioned in the ancient Hindu text, the *Garuda Purana*) and the birthplace of Lord Krishna.

above:
An aerial photo of Mathura city with Potra Kund in the foreground and the Yamuna at the back

right:
Black marble idol of infant Krishna at the Dwarkadheesh Temple

Some of the famous temples in the city of Mathura are:

The Krishna Janamsthan Temple: A city landmark, visible from the Delhi–Agra Highway as it passes Mathura, the temple has been built on the site of the Keshav Dev Temple built by the Raja of Orchha near the *Potra Kund,* a sacred water tank during the reign of the Mughal emperor Jahangir in the 17th century. Destroyed by Aurangzeb in 1669, the drive for its reconstruction gained momentum during the 1930s through a campaign led by the Hindutva leader and freedom fighter and Bharat Ratna awardee Madan Mohan Malaviya. The restoration began in 1951 and the temple was rebuilt by 1982 with financial help from donors that included the industrial houses of Birla, Dalmia and Goenka. The temple contains idols of Radha and Krishna in the sanctum sanctorum. Behind the sanctum is a chamber, said to be the prison of Kansa, where Lord Krishna took birth.

Dwarkadheesh Temple: The Dwarkadheesh Temple is one of the most visited among the temples in Mathura city. Located in the old quarter of the city, between Holi Gate and Vishram Ghat, the temple is known for its intricately carved Rajasthani-style architecture and exquisite paintings on the ceilings depicting episodes from the life of Lord Krishna. The temple was built in 1814 by a devotee with finance from the Scindia royalty of Gwalior (Madhya Pradesh). True to the tradition of the Vallabhacharya Sect, the idol is that of the infant Krishna made of black marble. Devotees throng the temple throughout the year, but the rush is particularly high during

the 13 day Hindola (swing) Festival in the monsoon season, one of the main festivals of the Pushti Margis, the followers of Vallabhacharya. During the festival, the idols of Krishna and Radha are placed on a golden swing for the devotees to rock as a demonstration of their love for the infant God.

The Birla/Gita Temple: Hinduism's holy book, the *Bhagwat Gita* (Eternal Song), was revealed by Lord Krishna to Arjuna during the Mahabharat battle. This temple was built by the industrialist Jugal Kishore Birla (1883–1967) in praise of the holy scripture in the year 1946. The temple's design is similar to that of other Birla temples in the country, with prominence given to the use of red and yellow ochre colours on the outside walls and lavish use of marble inside. The highlight of the temple is a tall pillar of red sandstone on the north side of the premises, with all 700 verses of the *Gita* inscribed on it. The temple is located on the outskirts of the city off the Mathura–Vrindavan road.

Vishram Ghat: A ghat is a place on a river bank or water tank used for various religious rituals, washing and bathing. Of the 25 ghats along the Yamuna River in Mathura–Vrindavan, the Vishram Ghat is considered the most sacred. Lord Krishna is believed to have taken rest (*vishram*) here after destroying Kansa. It is the main ghat of Mathura and also the starting and end point of the *84 kos Braj parikrama*. There are a number of small temples on the top such as the 18th century Gatishil Narain Temple, with steps leading down to the river. Vishram Ghat is a short distance from Holi Gate on the old Agra road. A picturesque 16th century tower, the Sati Burj, that marks

facing page above:
Close up of the verses inscribed on the Gita Stambh at the Birla Temple, Mathura

facing page below:
Gita Stambh at Birla Temple, Mathura

the site of a widow self-immolation (*sati*), is situated near the Ghat. For those wishing to avoid crowds, the best time to visit is sunrise or sunset when the devotees come to perform *aarti* (praying with little oil lamps).

Government Museum, Mathura: This is a museum with a striking collection of archeological finds, and is a must-see for all visitors to Mathura. It was founded in 1874 by the British District Collector F.S. Growse to safeguard and display the articles unearthed during several archaeological explorations undertaken in and around Mathura city. It contains a priceless collection of Buddhist and Jain sculptures dating from the 2nd century BCE in a style that has come to be known as the Mathura School of Sculpture which reached its zenith under the rule of the Kushanas.

Among the rare items is the oldest statue of Buddha ever found in the country and the only statue of the great Kushan king Kanishka whose empire stretched from Afghanistan to Pataliputra in India in the 2nd century CE. Most of the statues are of red spotted sandstone and some are huge, 12–13 feet in height and surprisingly well preserved.

The museum was origionally established in a beautiful building built of stone with a finely carved exterior on the old Agra Road which is now the Jain Museum. It was shifted to its present octagon-shaped premises in 1933 when it was known as the Curzon Museum of Archaeology. The Government Museum receives a large number of visitors, including pilgrims and tourists from Japan and other Buddhist countries of East and Southeast Asia.

facing page above:
Vishram Ghat, Mathura

facing page below:
Government Museum, Mathura

The first Buddha statue discovered, Mathura Museum

facing page above:
Krishna lifting Govardhan Hill, 7th century, Mathura Museum

facing page below:
Only statue ever found of Emperor Kanishka, 1st century, Mathura Museum

1. Name of the object:- Krishna Lifting

The City of Vrindavan

Vrindavan, Mathura's sister city, lies a few kilometers upstream on the Yamuna. Vrindavan literally means forest of *tulsi* (holy basil). In terms of religious sanctity, it ranks slightly higher than Mathura in the minds of Hindus. Its religious importance is due to the belief that Krishna spent much of his childhood and performed many of his miracles here. The city's river-front has a number of ghats or platforms with steps leading down to the river. The one highest upstream is called Kali Mardan Ghat, where Krishna is believed to have killed the serpent Kaliya; the one furthest downstream is called Kesi Ghat, marking the spot where a demon by the same name met a similar fate.

Kesi Ghat, Vrindavan

Vrindavan has been from the beginning a Hindu city, with no Buddhist or Jain archeological findings. It is also devoid of any significant Islamic monuments, even though the decree for establishing Vrindavan as a revenue village was issued by a Mughal emperor, Akbar. Unlike Mathura, which has a mix of administrative, military and religious establishments, Vrindavan is mainly spiritual in character, with numerous ashrams (religious retreats of holy men), *dharamshalas* (rest houses for pilgrims) and *gaushalas* (cow shelters). However, the main attraction of the city are its magnificent temples.

Madan Mohan Temple: This is the oldest extant temple of Vrindavan, established in the year 1534 by Sanatana Goswami, one of Chaitanya Mahaprabhu's first disciples. Built of red sandstone on a hillock near the Yamuna river bank at Kali Mardan Ghat, the temple is located on the Vrindavan Parikrama road. It has a distinct Nagara (North Indian) style architecture, standing on a stone platform with steps leading up to it and a high tower over the sanctum sactorum. The temple commands a panoramic view of the Yamuna River as well as of Vrindavan city. It is said that the temple's construction was financed by a trader from Multan, Ramdas Kapur, whose merchandise-carrying boat, marooned in the river, was freed after he prayed at the shrine of Madan Mohan (another name for Krishna) founded by the Goswami.

Madan Mohan Temple

Radha Raman Temple: This is also one of the seven old Goswami temples established in Vrindavan by the first disciples of Chaitanya Mahaprabhu. Here Krishna is worshipped as Radha Raman or the paramour of Radha. It is situated in the Raman Reti area, near Chir Ghat and was founded in 1542 by Gopal Bhatt Goswami whose *samadhi* (memorial) also lies in the temple's precincts. It is believed that the Goswami met Chaitanya Mahaprabhu as a child when the latter was touring the holy places of South India. The temple entrance has Rajasthan-style architecture with a *jharokha* (window) enclosed within a balcony and *jali* (lattice) work carved in stone. The "Mahamantra" is the main chant here as the shrine is managed by Gaudiya Vaishnavas (a sect founded by Chaitanya in Bengal). The present high priest of the temple is Shri Shrivatsa Goswami.

above:
Entrance of Radha Raman Temple

below:
Govind Dev Temple

Govind Dev Temple: One of Vrindavan's majestic medieval monuments, this has been called 'the most impressive religious structure that Hindu art has ever produced in Upper (north) India' by F.S. Growse in *Mathura: A District Memoir* (p. 61, 1874). The temple was built by Raja Man Singh of Amber (modern- day Jaipur) in 1590 over a shrine of Govindji (another of Krishna's synonyms) established by Rupa Goswami, Chaitanya Mahaprabhu's disciple. The imposing structure is made of high quality red sandstone, whose use was confined only to royal buildings in that (Mughal) era. The temple is three stories high and has an ornate mix of Hindu, Islamic, and western architecture. The original *shikhar* (spire) above the sanctum is said to have been demolished under the orders of the Mughal emperor Aurangzeb. The idols were shifted soon thereafter to the City Palace in Jaipur where they are still worshiped. The Govind Dev Temple is situated just off the main road that links Vrindavan to Mathura, close to several other historical sights of Vrindavan.

above:
Gopuram (entrance) to the Rangji Temple

facing page above:
Interior of the Govind Dev Temple

facing page below:
Entrance to the Bankey Bihari Temple

Rangji Temple: Rangji or Ranganath is how Vishnu (the Creator in the Hindu trinity) is known in the southern states of India. The Rangji Temple is situated close to the Govind Dev Temple in the heart of old Vrindavan and is dedicated to Lord Krishna, an incarnation of Vishnu. It is one of the few large temples in North India managed by the followers of the South Indian saint Ramanujan. It was built in 1853 by Radha Krishan and Govind Das, members of a rich banking family of Mathura who came under the influence of Swami Rangacharya, a great Sanskrit scholar and devotee of Ramanujan. The main building of the temple complex has a typical South Indian style architecture. A 10-day festival, the Brahmotsav, takes place in March in which the idol is placed on a huge wooden chariot which is pulled in a procession for a short distance from the temple, amidst much fanfare.

Bankey Bihari Temple: This temple belongs to the Haridas Sampraday or the descendents of Swami Haridas, the great saint, musician and devotee of Lord Krishna in the 16th century. The name has been derived partly from the shape of the idol which is bent at three places (*bankey*) and partly from *kunj vihari*, which was Haridas' way of referring to Krishna in his songs and poems. It is one of the most revered among

श्री धाम · वृन्दावन
श्री स्वामी हरिदास जी महाराज के वंशजों का निजी

all of Vrindavan's shrines and receives a flood of visitors throughout the year. The temple, built in 1863, has walls of red sandstone, with an intricately carved entrance gate made of white stone. The temple is approached through a narrow lane lined with shops selling flowers, sweets, garlands that are offered by the devotees at the temple. The location of the temple is Goda Vihar, a short distance from Nidhivan, the abode of Haridas.

Devotees thronging the Bankey Bihari Temple during Holi

Nidhivan today

Nidhivan: Situated in the Raman Reti area of Vrindavan, this is the location of the original *tulsi* (*vrinda* in Sanskrit) grove from which the city gets its name. Swami Haridas resided here and is said to have discovered the idol of Bankey Bihari which was later shifted to the temple of that name. A shrine dedicated to Haridas can be seen within the Nidhivan complex. According to legend, Nidhivan is the forest where Radha and Krishna used to perform the Raas Leela or the Dance of Divine Love. Hence it is regarded as one of the holiest spots in Vrindavan. The forested landscape now consists of *peelu* (salvadora persica) trees with gnarled trunks and branches. Movement of visitors is restricted to fixed paths which are covered with wire meshing as a protection against the troopes of monkeys that frequent the place.

above:
ISKCON Temple, Vrindavan

facing page above:
Haridas Shrine, Nidhivan

facing page below left:
Deities at Nidhivan

facing page below right:
Krishna and Balram idols in ISKCON Temple

ISKCON Temple: This is also called the Krishna-Balram Temple after the main idols installed there. It was built in 1975 under the guidance of A.C. Bhaktivedanta Swami Prabhupada, founder of the International Society for Krishna Consciousness (ISKCON, popular as the Hare Krishna sect). The temple has beautifully carved white marble architecture and idols. It receives a large number of visitors including a stream of devotees from abroad, many of whom stay in the residential complex available for ISKCON members. The rear portion of the complex which was the residence of Swami Prabhupada, has been converted into a museum showcasing his life and works. A restaurant, Govinda, offers pure vegetarian food to visitors. The temple is situated in the Raman Reti area of Vrindavan, along the *parikrama* route.

The Prem Mandir: A 21st century temple, the Prem Mandir is the latest addition to the long list of grand temples established in Vrindavan. A faithful follower of Radha-Krishna, the sage Jagatguru Kripaluji Maharaj got the temple built in 2012 as an offering of his devotion. Italian marble costing millions of dollars is said to have been used here. The multi-storeyed structure has marble floors with exquisite pietra dura inlay work. The area surrounding the temple is filled with gardens, fountains and life-sized scenes from the events in the Krishna legend. A light and sound show takes place in the evenings. The beauty, colour and grandeur of the Prem Mandir has made it one of the most visited sites for tourists in Vrindavan. The temple is situated on the Chhatikra Road, leading from NH 44 to Vrindavan city.

Prem Mandir, Vrindvan

Mathura's Satellite Towns

The holy land of Braj is not a well-defined administrative unit, but comprises the sacred forests, tanks and towns associated with the Krishna lore. Braj is centered around the twin cities of Mathura and Vrindavan which lie on the west bank of the Yamuna River. As it meanders from north to south, the river divides the district of Mathura into two broad halves. The land west of the Yamuna stretching to the border of Rajasthan is dry and has a few hilly tracts, around which are located the holy places of Govardhan and Barsana and, further north, the town of Kosi Kalan. The area east of the river which is more fertile, and where the topography is closer to that of the flatter alluvial Indo-Gangetic Doab (a land between two rivers), contains the temple towns of Gokul, Mahavan and Baldev.

Govardhan: Situated 22 km west of Mathura on the road to Deeg (Rajasthan), Govardhan is arguably the holiest town in Braj after Mathura and Vrindavan. It is separately accessible from Vrindavan via Radha Kund, a holy tank. According to the legend, the God of Rain, Indra, was furious with the people of Braj for failing to perform a *yajna* (vedic ritual done in front of a sacred fire accompanied by chants) in his honour. He vented his fury by sending a torrent of rain that inundated the land, causing rivers to overflow their banks so that it seemed that the people would be drowned in the deluge. Lord Krishna then came to their rescue by lifting the Govardhan Hill on his little finger, thereby shielding the land and the population from the storm. Ever since, Govardhan Hill (known as Giriraj Parvat locally) is worshiped as a manifestation of Krishna, and a pilgrimage is undertaken by the devotees all around the mountain. Though usually depicted as a conical structure in paintings of Lord Krishna,

below: *Govardhan Hill*

the Giriraj Parvat is actually an elongated rocky outcrop that rises abruptly from the flatland and stretches in a south westerly direction for 7–8 km with an average height of 100 feet. The *parikrama* is around 22 km with numerous temples and water bodies enroute.

Kusum Sarovar, Govardhan

left:
Dan Ghati Temple, Govardhan

Among the most visited is the Dan Ghati (toll valley) Temple which is said to mark a spot where Krishna would tease the milkmaids crossing from one side of the Hill to the other by demanding a tax on their butter, cheese, curds and milk. Of the water bodies along the *parikrama*, the Mansi Ganga and Radha Kund are the most sacred, but the most picturesque is the Kusum Sarovar with its imposing *chhatri*s (pavilions) built in honour of the great Jat ruler Suraj Mall and his queens, who died in 1764 fighting the Rohillas, a tribe of Pashtun (Afghan) origin who had grown powerful with the decline in the authority of the Mughals.

Barsana: The town of Barsana is situated 40 km from Vrindavan and 20 km from Govardhan. It is believed to be the birth place of Radha, the consort of Lord Krishna. The town is located on the base of a hill on which a series of temples dedicated to Radha (Ladliji or 'beloved' in local parlance) have been built over the centuries. The latest of the hill top temples, the Radharani Temple, was built in the 18th century and is accessible by a stone staircase from the foot of the hill. In recent times, two new magnificent

Radha Rani Temple, Barsana

temples, the Rangeeli Mahal (1996) and the Kirti Mandir (2012) have come up on the plains below, courtesy the sage Kripaluji Maharaj, with landscaped gardens, waterfalls, prayer halls, and a charitable hospital.

However, the chief attraction of Barsana is the world famous Lathmaar (literally 'stick beating') Holi which takes place 11 days prior to the date of the actual festival. Men from the neighbouring town of Nandgaon, wearing colourful turbans and carrying protective shields arrive at Barsana

Kirti Mandir, Barsana

where they are met in the main market square by local damsels, faces veiled to prevent identification, carrying thick wooden staffs. Amidst the beating of drums and the roar of onlookers, rustic taunts are exchanged between the two sides after which the women start beating their adversaries, landing heavy blows with their staffs, while the men try and shield themselves. The mock fight spectacle lasts for much of the morning and draws thousands of spectators and tourists, who watch the proceedings closely packed in every nook and corner of the square or swarming on the rooftops and balconies of the surrounding houses. An identical battle takes place in Nandgaon the following day, this time between turbaned and colour-drenched men visiting from Barsana and the local Nandgaon lasses wielding their *lathis*.

Kosi Kalan: This is the first town in the district of Mathura one encounters when travelling from Delhi on the historic Grand Trunk road (now National Highway 44). A sub-divisional headquarters, Kosi, situated 44 km from Mathura, has both historical and spiritual importance. During Mughal times, it was a resting place for travellers with a caravan-*serai* of considerable size. During the 1857 War of Independence, rebel sepoys had fortified themselves within the *serai* for some time before they were ejected by a British expeditionary force specially sent from Agra. An important site of spiritual importance lies a few kms down the road towards Nandgaon/ Barsana where a Shani Temple exists with a 50 ft high statue of Shani Dev. This temple is in the middle of a wooded area called Kokilavan linked to the Radha Krishna legend. The temple is visited especially on Saturdays (*Shanivar* in Hindi) by hundreds of devotees from near and far who come to pray to ward off evil and overcome personal obstacles.

Shani statue, Kosi

महाप्रभुश्रीमद्वल्लभाचार्यचरण सुत
श्रीविट्ठलेशात्मज
श्रीगोकुलनाथजी कौ घर

Gokul: According to legend, Gokul marks the place where Vasudev handed over the baby Krishna to his foster father Nand to save him from the evil designs of his uncle, the cruel king Kansa. It is also the place where Vallabhacharya first came to Braj as a child accompanying his parents who had been displaced from Varanasi. In due course, as his philosophy spread, Gokul was made the headquarters of the Vallabhacharya Sampraday (sect). It receives a huge number of pilgrims, many of them from Gujarat where the sect has the maximum following. Numerous temples have been built on the river bank and one of the most revered is the Gokulnathji Temple, built in the 19th century and named after one of Acharya's descendants. Gokul lies on the 84 *kos braj parikrama* and is the last point of halt on the route before pilgrims return to the yatra's starting point at Vishram Ghat in Vrindavan. The town is situated downstream around 9 km from Mathura and can be accessed by the road bridge over the Gokul barrage on the Yamuna which was completed in 2003 to augment the city water supply.

Mahavan: A short distance inland from Gokul lies the sub-divisional headquarters of Mahavan. There is some indication that it was the most important town of Braj next to Mathura at one point in history and was looted by Mahmud of Ghazni during his sacking of Mathura in 1017. The name Mahavan means 'Great Forest'. Though the area is bare now, it is said that a large forest existed here at one time where the Mughal emperor Shah Jahan shot four tigers during a tiger hunt in the year 1634. According to belief, this is where Yashoda

facing page above:
Aerial view of Gokul town on the Yamuna

facing page below:
Shri Gokulnathjikou Ghar

above:
Chaurasi Khamba Temple, Mahavan

facing page:
Huranga Holi, Baldev

gave birth to the girl child Yogmaya who was exchanged for baby Krishna six days after his birth. The exchange is said to have taken place at a spot close to the Chaurasi Khamba (84 pillar) Temple, which is the main attraction for pilgrims coming to Mahavan. The pillars have a design similar to those found in the Qutub Minar complex in Delhi, an indication that they may have been sculpted around the 10th century CE. The rush of pilgrims is at its peak on the occasion of Sri Krishna Janmashtami (birthday). Mothers come here to perform the *chhati puja* (ritual done six days after childbirth) of Lord Krishna. Mahavan is also where the siblings Lord Krishna and his brother Balram grew up under the care of foster parents Yashoda and Nand. According to folklore, it is also the site where the demoness Pootna was destroyed by the infant Krishna.

Baldev: Situated east of Mahavan on the road leading to Sadabad, Baldev town is 23 km from Mathura city. Legend says that it is the place where Balram, Lord Krishna's elder brother (*dauji* in Braj Bhasha) was born. The chief attraction in Baldev is the Dauji Temple situated next to the Kshirsagar tank from where, according to folklore, a statue of Balram was recovered around 1535 following a dream had by Gosain Gokulnath, a direct descendant of Vallabhacharya. Baldev is known for its Huranga (no holds barred) Holi, celebrated two days after the actual festival which draws thousands of pilgrims and tourists. The celebrations, held within the precincts of the Dauji temple and the adjacent by-lanes and alleys, rank next to only the Lathmaar Holi of Barsana in intensity and fervour.

Festivals and Parikramas of Mathura

Mathura is a land of festivals and festivities. There is hardly any day in the year when a religious celebration does not take place in a temple, or around some *ghat* or sacred tank. Some of its important festivals are described below:

Holi

The paramount festival of Mathura is Holi, the festival of colours. This ancient festival is the gift of the Radha-Krishna legend to the culture of India. According to the story, an adolescent Krishna, being of a dark complexion, was unsure if the fair Radha would accept him. As a solution, Mother Yashoda asked him to darken Radha's face by smearing any colour he liked. Thus began a tradition that continues till today of applying colours as a way of expressing friendship and affection between friends.

In most places, Holi is a two-day festival that takes place in February–March. In Mathura, Holi is a 45-day affair and festivities begin from Basant Panchami which marks the onset of spring (mid-February). There are different types of Holi celebrations that take place in different towns and temples of Mathura on different days. The most famous celebrations are the Lathmaar (stick beating) Holi of Barsana, replicated the next day at Nandgaon; the Phool Wali (flowers) Holi

Lathmaar Holi, Barsana

staged at various dance festivals during the festival season; and the Huranga (rowdy) Holi at the town of Baldev. Many temples in Mathura and Vrindavan hold community Holi celebrations where throngs of devotees are sprayed coloured water by priests from *pichkari*s or water pistons. There is also a colourful Holi procession taken out in Mathura city from Vishram Ghat to Holi Gate.

Chhoti (Little) Holi: Chhoti Holi, marked by the lighting of bonfires, is celebrated a day before the main Holi festival. According to the legend, the treacherous king Hiranyakashyap issued a command that all should worship

him and no other. However, the god-fearing Prahlad defied these commands and continued to worship Lord Vishnu, the Preserver in Hinduism's trinity of gods. The king had a wicked sister Holika who had a boon that she could not be burnt by fire. Infuriated by Prahlad's defiance, the king ordered that both Holika and Prahlad be made to sit on a blazing fire, in the expectation that Holika would survive the ordeal while he would be destroyed. In fact, due to the blessings of Vishnu, the opposite happened. Holika was set ablaze while Prahlad escaped unscathed. In most parts of north India, this incident is celebrated as Chhoti Holi, which symbolises the victory of good (Prahlad) over evil (Holika).

above:
Holi celebrations

facing page above:
Bonfire during Chhoti Holi in Falen

facing page below:
Idols of Prahlad and Holika

In Mathura, the main bonfire is lit on the square opposite Holi Gate, the entrance to the old part of the city. But an interesting twist to the festival can be witnessed in the town of Falen, 6 km east of Kosi Kalan, where a chosen priest (*panda*) runs and leaps through a gigantic burning bonfire in a live imitation of the survival of Prahlad in his ordeal by fire. This amazing performance takes place on Chhoti Holi in the heart of the town and witnessed by hundreds of awestruck onlookers gathered for the occasion.

Janamashthmi

Sri Krishna Janamashtmi ranks only next to Holi in terms of importance among the festivals of Mathura. Lord Krishna was born at midnight on the eighth day (*ashtmi*) of the month of *Bhadon* (August–September) in a prison cell. All over the district, this annual event is celebrated with the greatest festivity and joy in the hundreds of temples dedicated to Radha-Krishna. The most important Janamashtmi celebration takes place in the Krishna Janambhumi Temple which is the place where the prison cell is believed to have existed. The temple is specially lit up for the occasion. Its interior is decorated with flowers, lamps, garlands and flags. The idols of Krishna and Radha are bathed with milk and honey by the priests. A smell of burning incense sticks adds to the divine atmosphere. Devotees fast the whole day until the midnight hour. The event is telecast live for audiences all over the country.

Chunari Manorath

Thanksgiving rituals vary across cultures. In many societies, the ritual often involves an animal sacrifice. In Mathura, thanksgiving for a wish fulfilled (manorath) is performed in a unique manner—by 'draping' the river Yamuna in a *chunari* or saree. In Indian society, auspicious occasions are often marked by gifting sarees to the women in the household. Some believers regard the river Yamuna to be a female divine form, the *patrani* (chief queen) of Lord Krishna. Thus, a family whose wish has been fulfilled comes

facing page above:
Holi celebration at Dwarkadheesh Temple

भा.ज.पा.

to the river bank and offers a gift of sarees, whose number can vary from 31 to a 100 or more, to the Yamuna. These sarees are stitched together and carried across in boats from one bank of the river to the other, making a beautiful, colourful sight. Usually performed by Pushti Margis, the followers of Vallabhacharya, the ritual can be performed by anyone whose wish has been fulfilled, even outside the sect and on any day of the year.

Parikramas

In many religions, the act of walking around a sacred site is believed to bring great merit to a person. Depending on the intensity of devotion and the degree of merit desired, the *parikrama* (circumambulation) is undertaken at different levels of hardship by the devotees. Many walk barefoot but the most devout cover the distance by lying down prostrate pulling themselves forward, standing up and repeating the process (Dandavat Parikrama).

Dandavat Parikrama

Parikrama procession of sadhus

The 84 kos Braj Parikrama covers a distance of over 250 km and is the longest such pilgrimage. It starts from Vishram Ghat in Mathura and covers many temple towns, villages, sacred forests and sacred *kund*s (water tanks) all around the entire region of Braj, before ending at the Vishram Ghat itself. Along the route, the pilgrims can watch several musical dances and dramas based on the story of Lord Krishna, performed by local artistes. There is a marked similarity of this to the Jatras of Bengal, an indication one can presume, of the origins of the *parikrama*. The monsoon months of *Sawan* (July–August) are the best time for undertaking the 84 kos Braj Parikrama. Given the long route,

many pilgrims prefer to cover the distance by car, which is also acceptable.

The smaller, but popular 7 kos Govardhan Parikrama is a 21 kilometer km circuit around the Giriraj Hill in Govardhan. It starts from the Dan Ghati Temple and touches the sacred water bodies of Radha Kund, Mansi Ganga and Kusum Sarovar. The best time for this parikrama is the month of *Kartik* (October–November) as the mild autumn weather is conducive for pilgrims who want to perform the Dandavat *parikrama*, alternately prostrating themselves and standing up all the way.

There is also a shorter 5 kos Parikrama around Vrindavan. This takes 2–3 hours to complete and passes places of religious significance such as Kali Mardan Ghat, Madan Mohan Temple, Imli Tala, Kesi Ghat and several ashrams and *gaushala*s.

Finally, there is a 10 km long Mathura *parikrama* whose route passes city landmarks such as Kans Quila, Vishram Ghat, the Government Museum, the Kankali mound, Potra Kund, Krishna Janmasthan Temple and the Gayatri Tapobhumi. Traditionally, the most auspicious time to do this *parikrama* is on the full moon night of the month of *Baisakh* (April–May).

facing page:
Night parikrama

Saints and other Famous Inhabitants of Mathura, Ashrams, and Gaushalas

An ashram is usually the abode of a yogi or a holy man. It is a place where he stays, prays and meets his devotees. After his death, it often becomes a place of pilgrimage for his devotees and disciples. A large number of ashrams in Mathura and Vrindavan have been established in the name of such *sadhus*, *sadhvis* and other religious figures. The Ramkrishna Mission Seva Ashram runs a large charitable hospital in Vrindavan with specialist doctors visiting from Delhi. Some other ashrams are those of Swami Haridas named Kunj Kuti at Nidhivan, Vrindavan; Neem Karoli Baba's ashram at Atalla Chungi, Vrindavan; Pandit Shriram Sharma's Gayatri Tapobhumi, Mathura; Jai Gurudev (NH 44, Mathura), Ma Anandmayee (opposite

Ramkrishna Mission hospital, Vrindavan) and Sadhvi Rithambara's Vatsalya Gram, Vrindavan.

Vrindavan also has a large number of ashrams for widows. It is said that Chaitanya Mahaprabhu had exhorted them to come to Vrindavan and follow the path of devotion to Sri Krishna. For many years now, elderly women who hail mostly from Bengal have been living in homes attached to temples or set up by charitable trusts or by the government, where their food, clothing and shelter needs are taken care of. The social service organisation Sulabh International has been celebrating Diwali and Holi with them for the past few years, besides providing financial aid and compassionate care.

Saints and other famous inhabitants of Mathura

Throughout its history, Mathura has been the *janam bhumi* (place of birth) or the *karma bhumi* (place of deeds) of numerous lofty personalities, who have left an indelible mark on its character and its way of life. Many such persons have been influenced by the story of Lord Krishna for whom Mathura was both *janam bhumi* as well as *karma bhumi*. Some of these have themselves influenced the very narrative of Krishna as it is understood in the Braj region today. Others, whose main belief may have centered on another deity like Lord Rama or Hanuman, found the religious environment of Mathura–Vrindavan congenial for dwelling permanently or even spending their last days there. A brief characterisation of 10 such luminaries follows, in

facing page:
Vrindavan widows setting off on a Diwali procession

chronological order:

Vallabhacharya (1479–1531): Vallabhacharya was born in a Telegu family that lived in Varanasi. He was one of the saints of the Bhakti movement of medieval India which aimed to universalise the worship of God among the masses by introducing simplicity in Hindu religious practices. Having mastered the Vedas and other religious texts at a very young age, he became a devout worshiper of Lord Krishna. He set out to visit all the holy places of the country and stayed for

a while in Mathura where he ordained his first disciple in 1493 before returning to Varanasi. His teachings, known as the Pushti Marg, center on the worship of Bal Gopal (infant Krishna) and have a considerable following within the business communities of Rajasthan and Gujarat. The blind classical poet Surdas who wrote devotional poetry dedicated to Lord Krishna in Braj Bhasha was also a follower of Vallabhacharya. The Dwarkadheesh Temple in Mathura, the Gokulnath Temple in Gokul and the Srinathji Temple in Nathdwara (Rajasthan) have been built by his followers, the Vallabhacharya Sampradaya.

Chaitanya Mahaprabhu (1486–1534): Enormous credit for the surge of Krishna worship in the Mathura–Vrindavan-Braj region goes to Chaitanya Mahaprabhu and his immediate disciples. Born Vishambhar Misra in Nadia, Bengal, he was a leading light of the Bhakti movement and founder of the Gaudiya Vaishnava Sampradaya, the Krishna-centric movement of Bengal. A distinguishing feature of Chaitanya's teachings is that one can attain unison with God by simply reciting his name without any added prayer. To this end, he promoted the Mahamantra (the Great Chant): 'Hare Krishna Hare Krishna, Krishna Krishna Hare Hare; Hare Rama Hare Rama, Rama Rama, Hare Hare'. Chaitanya travelled throughout India to spread his message and visited Vrindavan around 1515 CE. Later, after returning to Bengal, he sent several of his disciples, including Goswamis Rupa, Sanatana and Gopal Bhatt to Vrindavan to establish shrines for the worship of Lord Krishna. The Madan Mohan Temple,

facing page:
Dwarkadheesh Temple, Mathura

Radha Raman Temple and the Govind Dev Temple, all revered shrines in Vrindavan today were founded by the Goswamis. Among the prominent modern gurus inspired by Chaitanya Mahaprabhu are Swami A.C. Bhaktivedanta Prabhupada (founder of the Hare Krishna movement) and Kripaluji Maharaj. Imli Tala, a temple dedicated to Chaitanya Mahaprabhu, is situated near Kesi Ghat, Vrindavan.

Swami Haridas: There is some confusion about the exact dates of his birth and death, but it is known that Swami Haridas, the great spiritual poet and musician flourished (and died) during the reign of the Mughal emperor Akbar (1556–1605). A celibate, he lived in his ashram at Nidhivan, now one of Vrindavan's holiest places, where he taught classical music and tutored two of medieval India's fabled musicians and singers Tansen and Baiju Bawra. A devout worshipper of Lord Krishna, who he called 'Kunj Vihari', he wrote and sang songs about the love between Radha and Krishna. His descendants, Goswamis of the Haridas Sampraday, founded and maintain one of Vrindavan's most revered shrines, the Bankey Bihari Temple. A shrine devoted to Swami Haridas can be found in Nidhivan, in the Raman Reti area, near the Bankey Bihari Temple.

Frederick Salmon Growse (1836–1893): A member of the Indian Civil Service during British rule in India, he combined the talents of an administrator, archaeologist, scholar, architect and Indologist. F.S. Growse was Joint Magistrate/Collector of Mathura district from 1870–1876.

Imli Tala, Vrindavan

He had a profound love and understanding of Hindi and its dialects—Awadhi and Braj Bhasha—and was the first person who translated Tulisidas' *Ramcharitmanas* (the classic religious text written in Awadhi) into English which was published in installments from 1876–1883. He carried out several excavations in Mathura which unearthed the Buddhist and Jain history of the city. The Government Museum of Mathura was founded in 1874 in a building designed by him. It now houses the Jain Museum of Mathura. He is also the author of *Mathura - A District Memoir,* a fascinating account of Braj, its history, its culture, its monuments and people. First published in 1876, it is

above:
Jain Museum, Mathura

facing page above:
F.S. Growse

facing page below:
Intricate wall panelling of the Jain Museum, Mathura

regarded as a model for district gazetteers. Growse designed and built the Sacred Heart Church of Mathura and also several buildings in Bulandshahr, a neighbouring district in Uttar Pradesh, where he was posted as Collector, after being transferred from Mathura.

A.C. Bhaktivedanta Swami Prabhupada (1896–1977): Born Abhay Chandra De in Kolkata in a family of Gaudiya Vaishnavas, he was a devout worshipper of Lord Krishna in the Chaitanya tradition. Having studied in an elite educational institution, the Scottish Church College, Kolkata, he was one of the first Hindu preachers to propagate worship of Krishna in the English language. He lived in Vrindavan from 1950 till 1965 when he moved to the USA where he founded the International Society for Krishna Consciousness (ISKCON) in New York City in 1966. He soon attracted a huge following, both in India and abroad. His disciples can be seen chanting the Mahamantra in unison while dancing in ecstasy in and around various cities in different parts of the world. ISKCON has a large number of temples which are known for their neat and clean appearance and beautiful idolatry. Besides Krishna worship, ISKCON is also engaged in social, educational and charitable activities. Its overseas centres run free kitchens (*langars*/*bhandaras*) where eminent people like Steve Jobs (co-founder of Apple) were known to be frequent visitors.

Swami Prabhupada died in Vrindavan and his *samadhi* is in the Krishna Balram (ISKCON) Temple situated in the Raman Reti area, on the Vrindavan Parikrama Road.

Neem Karoli Baba (1900–1973): Originally Lakshman Narain Sharma from Firozabad district of Uttar Pradesh, he is named after Nib Karori, a village in Farrukhabad district of Uttar Pradesh, where he supposedly stopped a train using his mystic powers. A devotee of Lord Hanuman, he preached that *seva* to the poor is the best way to serve God. His simple, rustic, spiritual personality attracted lakhs of followers, including several well-known American personalities like Mark Zuckerberg (co-founder Facebook/Meta). Another prominent disciple was Richard Alpert, a Harvard University professor, who wrote the bestseller *Be Here Now* and became Baba Ram Das, after meeting the saint. For the last 10 years of his life Neem Karoli Baba mostly stayed in his ashram at Kainchi, near Nainital, Uttarakhand, which is thronged by thousands of his followers on 15 June every year, marking the day when a Hanuman temple was erected there in 1964. He died in Vrindavan. His ashram, situated on Atalla Chungi Road in Vrindavan, was established in 1967 and contains his *samadhi* (final resting place).

Acharya Shriram Sharma (1911–1990): Born in Agra district, he was a widely admired spiritual teacher who lived in Mathura from the 1950s to 1971 before moving to Haridwar (Uttarakhand) where he ultimately passed away. He founded the Gayatri Parivar, which has millions of

Gayatri Tapobhumi, Vrindavan

followers who believe in the spiritual power of chanting the Gayatri mantra, a sacred chant from the *Rig Veda*, used in meditation and prayers. He also founded the Yug Nirman Yojana, a movement to improve societal values worldwide, which has branches in dozens of countries abroad. A prolific writer on Hindu religious texts, he also gave advice on day-to-day individual and family living through his *Akhand Jyoti* monthly magazine which has been published from Mathura without break since 1941. His ashram in Mathura, called

Gayatri Tapobhumi, which he set up in 1950 is located off the Mathura–Vrindavan road.

Pandit Deendayal Upadhyaya (1916–1966): He was born in Nagla Chandrabhan village 4 kilometers from Farah town on the Mathura–Agra Highway and 24 km from Mathura city. One of the senior-most ideologues of the Rashtriya Swayamsewak Sangh (RSS), the Hindu nationalist body, he launched the weekly Panchjanya magazine in 1948 in Lucknow. He was seconded by the RSS to the Jan Sangh (precursor to the Bharatiya Janata Party) soon after it was founded by Shyama Prasad Mukherji in 1951 and functioned as its national general secretary for 15 years. He became President of the Jan Sangh in 1967 but his tenure was cut short by his untimely demise in 1968 in Mughal Sarai railway station near Varanasi (now renamed Deendayal Upadhyaya junction). A Deen Dayal Dham (place of pilgrimage) has been developed at his birthplace in Mathura district with a memorial, a Saraswati Vidya Mandir (inter-college) and Ayurveda dispensary.

Deoraha Baba (? –1990): Originally hailing from Deoria district in eastern Uttar Pradesh, he lived much of his life in Vrindavan, staying on a *machan* (raised platform) on the banks of the Yamuna River. An enigmatic mystic, who preached the glory of Lord Rama, cow worship, he was known as the 'ageless Yogi'. People from all walks of life came to seek his blessings, including India's first President Dr Rajendra Prasad and Prime Minister Indira

Deoraha, Baba Memorial, Vrindavan

Gandhi. His *machan* and *samadhi* can be seen from Kesi Ghat in Vrindavan on the directly opposite bank of the Yamuna.

Jagatguru Kripaluji Maharaj (1922–2013): Born near Kunda in Pratapgarh district of Uttar Pradesh in a Tripathi Brahmin family, he moved to Vrindavan at age 16 and became greatly influenced by the teachings of Chaitanya. He spent the rest of his life devoted to worshiping Lord Krishna and his consort Radha, in particular the latter. A gifted speaker, he had time slots for his speeches across several spiritual television channels in India and earned millions of dedicated followers. Later in life he lived in Barsana, the birthplace of Radha, where he constructed two

beautiful temples called Rangeeli Mahal and Kirti Mandir (named after the mother of Radha). He also built a temple complex in Austin, Texas, USA. His piece de resistance is the exquisite Prem Mandir (Temple of Love) in Vrindavan, built of expensive Italian marble which has become one of the main attractions of the city today, especially for young people. After his passing, his teachings continue to be disseminated through Jagatguru Kripalu *parishad*s (councils) throughout India and abroad.

Gaushalas

Cows have been venerated in India from ancient times. Lord Krishna came from a family of cowherds and one of his holy names is 'Gopal', meaning one who tends to cows. According to *Garuda Puran*, the Hindu scripture, Lord Krishna exhorted his fellow cowherds thus: *Maddai vatam viddhi giriyasca vananic* i.e. 'We, cowherds, live in forests. Our life is sustained by the wealth of cows. Therefore, cows, hills and forests are our gods'.

Ramesh Baba Gaushala

In the land of Krishna, the protection of this sacred animal is believed to bring special merit to the protector. It is not surprising then, that the district of Mathura is replete with *gaushala*s or cow shelters. The Maan Mandir Sewa Trust of Ramesh Baba hosts thousands of homeless cows in its shelters. Established in 2007 in Barsana from a grant sent by an anonymous NRI in the US, the *gaushala* has its own veterinary hospital with an ICU manned by a team of skilled veterinarians and giant hangars for stockpiling the thousands of tonnes of animal feed required for the daily feed of the cows. For his services, Ramesh Baba received India's fourth highest civilian award, the Padma Shri, in 2019.

Radha Surabhi Gaushala

Mahatma Gandhi called cow protection 'Hinduism's gift to the world'. One Westerner who found the idea of cow protection worthy of adoption is Friederike Irina Bruning from Germany, who has been running a *gaushala* near Radha Kund, Barsana for the past two decades. Now known as

Mata Sudevi with her cows

Sudevi, she had come from Berlin to Vrindavan 45 years ago in order to lead a spiritual life. By chance, she came across an injured cow which she took home and nursed back to health. Thus began a saga of sheltering and nursing cows that were hurt in accidents, sickened by disease, attacked by animals or otherwise abandoned. As the numbers grew, she managed to buy a piece of land where she set up the Radha Surabhi Gaushala near Barsana, Mathura. On a visit to the Gaushala one comes across cows with accident injuries, including leg fractures, cows that have suffered attacks by stray dogs and cows that are blind. Mata Sudevi, who can be called the 'Mother Theresa of cows', was also conferred the Padma Shri in 2019.

Cuisine of Mathura

The food of any land is the culmination of time-honoured customs, centuries of change and influences, climate and religion. So it is with Braj. Being the birthplace of Lord Krishna, also on the path of foreign invaders, the pilgrim towns of Mathura–Vrindavan and the region of Braj, have assimilated food influences from travellers, pilgrims, invaders, and offered their own to the outside world. The food traditions are said to be age-old from the time of Krishna, *satvik* (vegetarian food, without the use of onions and garlic), and milk and dairy dominant.

Fasting foods

Cultures all over the world teach abstinence from food for short or long periods. There may be many a rationale behind the practice, but the common ones are to teach endurance, sacrifice one's desires, or to acclimatise the body to changing seasons, detoxing the body to maintain a balance of the *doshas* , and sustainability for Mother Earth. For instance, by not consuming some of nature's produce, we give it time for regeneration.

facing page:
A stack of the famous Mathura pedas

In India, the fasting calendar varies from region to region and religion to religion. But in the Braj region, the main fasting days are Ekadashi, Maha Shivratri, Navratri, and Janmashtami. These periods of fasting permit certain foods that can be consumed, which are mainly fruits and dairy, nuts and flour made from non-cereals, such as lotus seeds, water-chestnuts and amaranth seeds. Barnyard millet is often used as a substitute for rice. Rock salt is permitted, as are some root vegetables and gourds. Since grains and lentils are not permitted, the above-mentioned flours are used for making *puri*s, and desserts like *halwa* and *kheer*. With the availability of potato flour, even *jalebi*s are available for the fasting populace. In fact, *aloo ki jalebi* is a local speciality. Restaurants and street shops also feature *phalahari thali* during periods of fasting, such as Navratri. A *vrat* (fasting) *thali* may have dishes like *aloo jhol*, *dahi arvi*, *kaddu ki subzi*, *sabudana khichdi*, *sama ke chawal ki kheer*, *phal ka raita* and *kootu ki puri*. During the Ekadashi fast, the permitted food is consumed after sunset. During other fasts, there is flexibility of mealtimes, but usually one meal after sunset is the norm. During the day fruits, nuts and milk are permitted.

Bhog or Temple Food

Patram, pushpam, phalam toyam
yo may bhaktya prayachhati
Tadaham bhaktyupahritam
shami prayatatmanah.

('The reverent presentation to Me of a leaf, a flower, a fruit, or water, given with pure intention, is a devotional offering especially pleasing to me')

Bhagawad Gita (9.27)

Food offered to the deities is called *bhog*. In keeping with the above sentiment expressed by Lord Krishna, *bhog* is

Chhappan bhog laid out for the deity

offered to the deities with devotion and the *bhava* ('intent') to please the Lord. The temples of Mathura and Vrindavan are known for their Bhog Seva (service), and an elaborate food offering of 56 items called Chhappan Bhog. Temples have their own sanitised kitchens to prepare *bhog* for their deity. Notable among them are the Sri Bankey Bihari Temple and the Sri Radha Raman Temple, where the fire, on which *bhog* is prepared, is said to be over 450 years old, ignited by Vedic chants, and has been continuously burning since. The principles of Vedic cooking are followed in the preparation of the food for the deities. Fresh ingredients, and incorporating all the six *Rasas* (tastes)—astringent, bitter, pungent, salty, sour and sweet, in every meal, are some of the rules followed by the *sewayat*s (cooks offering their services to the deity). The *sewayat*s must bathe before entering the kitchen and can leave only after preparing the complete meal. The food is never tasted before being offered as *bhog*. It is always *satvik* as this promotes *satvik guna*s (pure qualities). It is believed that food is not only for nutrition but also influences the mind and consciousness in both Ayurveda and Yoga traditions.

The offering can range from tulsi (holy basil) leaves, water, milk to Chhappan Bhog or more. Two tulsi leaves are placed on all the food offered to Lord Krishna. Songs or *Pada* (a unit of poetic meter) are sung while offering *bhog* to the deity.

Aao bhog lagao mere Mohan,
Aisan bhog lagao mere Mohan,
Sab Amrit ban jaye mere Mohan

('Come and partake of the bhog Mohan [another name of Krishna]
Partake of it in such a manner,
That everything turns to nectar')

When *bhog* is offered, the doors of the temple are generally closed, and curtains are drawn. During this period, the food is said to receive the blessings of the deity. It is then distributed as *prasad* to the devotees, and the partaking of it establishes the relationship with God. This offering of food as *bhog* and its consumption as *prasad*, is central to the practice of *puja* (worship).

In many temples of Mathura and Vrindavan, *bhog* is offered eight times a day, once for each *prahar* (a unit of time, approximating to three hours). It is also known as the 'Ashtayam Seva', by Pushti Margis as well as the followers of the Radha Vallabh sect of Vaishnavites. Just as a child is fed at small intervals, the infant Krishna is given eight food offerings in a day. A vast array of food and drinks are prepared for each *prahar*—*laddoo*s, *mathri*s and *kachori*s for breakfast; sweets of different kinds; lentils, curries, rice and *roti*s for lunch or *rajbhog*; scented water, *boondi*, *sev* for evening snack; chopped fruits of various kinds; and *poori*s, *kachori*s, *saag* and vegetables for dinner, are a typical day's offering at the temples. There is also a tradition of offering *paan* (betel leaf), stuffed with dry fruits and *misri* (sugar candy) to the deity after each meal.

The selection of each dish is guided by the seasonal produce, and what agrees with the constitution during the certain month. For instance, *lassi* (a yoghurt drink) and *thandai* (a sweet milk and spice-based drink) are offered during the summer months, warm saffron infused milk during winter. Fruits and vegetables of the season; *halwa* for winter, *dahi vada*, and *rabri* in summer, *ghewar* during the monsoon season. Festivals too, determine the *bhog* menu—*makhan misri* at Janmashtami, *gujia* and *thandai* for Holi, *kheer* for Sharad Purnima, *arvi* (colocassia) for Radha Ashtami, *annakoot ki tarkari* for Annakoot, are some examples. The *makhan misri prasad* of the Bankey Bihari Temple is famous, as is the Kulhiya Prasad of the Radha Raman Temple.

At home, devotees offer whatever they cook such as *bhog* to the deity before consuming it as *prasad*. It can be a simple rice and lentil meal or a lavish one. What is important is the *bhava* (sentiment) with which it is cooked and offered.

During special festivals, the tradition of offering Chhappan Bhog is followed in most Krishna temples in India and abroad. The story behind this elaborate food offering goes thus: the village folk of Vrindavan used to offer lavish feasts to appease the weather God Indra. Lord Krishna asked the villagers to stop the practice, and worship the Govardhan Hill, the forests and the river that sustain them and their cattle. Angered by this, Lord Indra sent down incessant torrential rain for seven days. On seeing the plight of the villagers, Lord Krishna offered the people of Braj protection from the downpour by lifting the entire Govardhan Hill on His little finger, forming a huge canopy under which all the people and their cattle took shelter and were safe. After seven days Lord Indra realised his mistake and the rains stopped. It is said that Krishna did not eat for seven days while bearing the Govardhan Hill on His little finger. So as a gesture of gratitude to their saviour, the villagers prepared 56 dishes, one for each *prahar* of the day, for seven days, and offered them as Chhappan Bhog to their Protector, Lord Krishna and the Govardhan Hill. As it was the day after Diwali, this practice is observed as Govardhan Pooja, also known as Annakoot (mountain of food).

Goddess Laxmi is said to preside over the kitchen during the preparation of Chhappan Bhog. There can be many variations of the *bhog* menu. The three broad categories of food offered to the deity, are milk and milk products, such as *makhan misri*, *kheer*, *peda*, *lassi* etc.; the other category is flour- and *ghee*- (clarified butter) based, deep fried, sweet or saltless preparations; the third category is rice, lentils, vegetables etc. Once the *bhog* is cooked, it is served in metal or leaf-fabricated plates or bowls. Arranged in a set order, the dishes are placed before the deity in three groups. The sweet milk and milk preparations are placed on the right side of the deity, the flour-based preparations, to the left, and the rest of the food is placed in the centre.

Bhog is regularly prepared in the temple kitchens by cooks who strictly follow cleanliness and hygiene guidelines. The medium of cooking is *ghee*, and the milk is sourced from affiliated *gaushala*s for assured purity and quality. Devotees can pay for Bhog Seva too by sponsoring the *bhog* at any *prahar* or day. In most homes too, daily home food is offered to the *vigraha* (idol) before consumption. The same practice is followed in all ashrams, even the widow ashrams, where food is synonymous with *prasad*. This relationship of the devotees with the Divine through food is a way to express devotion and gratitude for His grace and benefaction.

It is worth noting that the delicacies offered to the deities have had a spill-over effect, and some food like *peda, rabri, kachoris* and *thandai* have become popular street-fare. The temple kitchens cook limited quantities, leaving devotees hankering for more. So entrepreneurs have pitched in to satiate the public palate, and have specialised in what they offer.

facing page:
Assembly line of cooks making the famous pedas in the Chowk area of Mathura

Mathura Peda

The mention of Mathura, instantly brings to mind the special *peda*, which is the geo-speciality sweet of this city. This *peda* has a long association with Mathura. Though the origin of the Mathura *peda* is shrouded in mystery, the Krishna lore may offer some clues. It is said that when Krishna was a toddler, He was caught eating mud. On being reprimanded by Mother Yashoda, He opened His mouth, and to her amazement, she saw a glimpse of the entire universe (*Brahmand*) in His little mouth. At a Krishna temple at Brahmand Ghat in the nearby town of Gokul, where this incident is believed to have occurred, *peda*s made of *raj* (mud) are sold for *bhog*, and distributed as *prasad* to the devotees. To the devotees, even the dirt of Braj is sacred, as their

Lord tread the land. Legend has it that Mother Yashoda used to prepare the caramelised *peda* by cooking down milk in an earthen pot, on a slow cow-dung cake fire, till the milk solids acquired a rich, golden brown hue. Krishna is believed to have loved the sweet.

We find references to the peda in ancient texts too, where it is referred to as *dugdha pindaka*. *Dugdha* means milk and *pind* or *pindaka* are Sanskrit words, meaning a lump of food. The *Charaka Samhita*, an ancient Sanskrit text on Ayurveda, written by Charaka, and the *Bhojanakutuhalam*, a 17th century Sanskrit text on the benefits of Ayurveda, mention it as a nutrient-dense recipe, suitable for persons desirous of weight gain and instant energy.

A visit to the kitchens of the famous Brijwasi Factory in the Chowk area of the city, where the Mathura *peda* is mass-produced, is a lesson in ancient gastronomy. Gallons of milk are boiled, and then cooked down to a solid state, which is called *khowa* or *mawa*. Then it is constantly stirred in huge cast-iron *kadhai*s (spherical, concave cooking vessels), on slow fire for hours, till the desired golden brown colour is achieved. It is then emptied in huge sheet-pans to cool, and *tagar* (fine crystalised sugar) and cardamom powder are added and mixed well. It is transferred to big vessels and , when cool enough to handle, rows of cooks, pinch small, lemon-sized balls, slightly flattening them, and toss them on to trays with more tagar, for dusting them, then they are sent to outlets for sale.

The local residents remember Totaram Halwai shop as the oldest one for *peda*s, but now numerous shops sell

pedas, the favourite sweet of Mathura. Tourists and pilgrims throng the shops to take away a sweet memory of Mathura. Presidents and prime ministers, too, are said to have had a weakness for this delicacy from Krishna's home town.

Street food

Milk

The economy of Mathura and the stories of Krishna revolve around cows and milk. Every morning, the streets of Mathura–Vrindavan wake up to the smell of boiling milk and the sound of ringing temple bells. Fresh raw-milk is placed in huge cast-

iron *kadhai*s, and boiled on slow coal fire. The aroma is both warming and comforting. For those who follow the *satvik* lifestyle, it is often the first warm drink of the day, as tea and coffee, being stimulants, are shunned by them. According to Ayurveda, milk has cooling properties. Warming a 'cold' food like milk, is said to promote nourishment and minimise the creation of toxic wastes. Winter is the time for warm, sweetened milk, sometimes flavoured with saffron and garnished with almond slivers, just as it is offered as *bhog* to the gods. In summer, boiled and cooled milk infused with saffron and cardamom, garnished with chopped almond and pistachio nuts, is preferred. The locals prefer to drink milk from street-corner shops where it is patiently cooked down on slow fires, till a thick layer of *malai* (skin of cream) forms on the surface, sweetened with unbleached sugar and served in small earthenware cups or *kulhad*. It is a good start to the day, and also, at night, a digestive and nightcap.

Lassi and Chhachh

Yoghurt is a popular milk product in the pilgrim town of Mathura. Set in large terracotta deep dishes, with a layer of *malai* on top, it is a good accompaniment to a meal, or as a dessert. Whipped with sugar, crushed ice and flavouring of rose or *kewra* (screwpine), it transforms into *lassi*, a divine yoghurt drink, also offered to deities in temples. It is similar to the 'Panchamrit' bhog offered at Janamashtami, and other occasions of worship. Lassi is a popular summer drink in the streets of Mathura–Vrindavan, providing respite from the searing summer heat, to pilgrims and travellers. Myriad shops line the temple streets, offering their own version. The 'Flying Lassiwala', Natthu Yadav at Chowk , is a current media sensation of sorts. He churns the lassi in a mixer, deftly tosses up a kulhad, pours the foamy liquid into it, topping it with malai, cardamom powder and rose syrup. Generally, the yoghurt used for lassi is made from buffalo milk, as it is thicker and creamier than cow milk.

Chhachh or buttermilk, is the residue obtained after churning whole milk and obtaining butter. It is a healthy

summer drink, often served with lunch. Tempered with *hing* (asafoetida) and cumin seeds, seasoned with plain or black salt, it has a cooling effect, and is good for the digestive system. Paintings of Mother Yashoda and other womenfolk of Gokul, churning milk in earthen pots to make butter, suggest its local origins and popularity.

Rabri and Khurchan

Rabri is another popular milk product of Mathura–Vrindavan. It is prepared by cooking down milk in large kadhais on slow coal fire, stirring intermittently until almost three-fourths of the milk evaporates, and a thick skin forms on the surface. It is lightly sweetened with sugar or *boora* (crystallised sugar), sometimes flavoured with saffron, and served cold.

Locals claim that rabri is Mathura's contribution to the world of desserts. The abundance of milk and the slow-fire cooking tradition has led to the invention this delicious dessert. It first finds mention in the *Chandimangala*, in the 15th century, according to the eminent food historian K.T. Achaya. It is believed that Lord Krishna is fond of this condensed milk preparation, so during the Ekadashi (11th day of the Moon) Bhog, *rabri* is almost mandatory in the temples of Vrindavan and Mathura.

Khurchan is the result when the milk is cooked in large shallow *kadhai*s on slow fire till all the liquid evaporates, leaving a layer of *malai* at the bottom. It is then scraped off, gently, in ribbons and curls, yielding *khurchan*, literally meaning scrapings. This is another famous delicacy of the Braj region. It is very delicate and mildly sweet, with a smoky flavour. It has a short shelf life, and is best eaten fresh.

Jalebi

Jalebi is a favourite breakfast dessert in most of North India. Each town has its own favourite *halwai* (sweetmeat maker), deftly swirling crisp *jalebi*s in piping hot *ghee* or oil, in flat bottomed *kadhai*s. The batter is a fermented mix of refined flour and water. Some add a little *besan* (gram flour) for colour and texture. After deep frying, the *jalebi*s are dipped in sugar syrup, removed and served in their crisp and syrupy glory. This dessert is said to have Arabic origins, but the *halwai*s in this region have made it their own. With small nano jalebis, or big jumbo *jaleba*s, locals are spoilt for choice. No breakfast is complete without this syrupy delight. After a spicy *kachori-aloo*, one instantly craves for this crispy sweet. Dunked in hot milk, or paired with cold *rabri*, it can be enjoyed in many ways.

Bhang and Thandai

With the onset of spring, Vrindavan and Mathura acquire a new colour. The dry terrain transforms into shades of green and yellow. The *tesu* (flame of the forest) trees redolent with bright saffron coloured blossoms, fields of roses and marigolds, green cannabis growing wild, lend the countryside a festive hue. Basant Panchmi is the festival of spring in India, and in Braj, it marks the commencement of Holi celebrations, lasting 45 days. *Bhang*, a drink made from the leaves and seeds of the cannabis plant, is the drink of the season here. Ancient Indian texts such as the *Rig Veda*, mention cannabis as an ingredient for the intoxicating drink *soma*; the *Sushruta Samhita* refers to it as a medicinal plant; in Ayurveda, it is used in concoctions for pain relievers and aphrodisiacs. It is considered by locals, to be an appetiser and a digestive.

Mythology refers to it as a favourite drink of Lord Shiva. Hence, during the festival of Mahashivratri, which falls in February-March between Basant Panchmi and Holi, *bhang* is offered as *bhog* in Shiva temples, and consumed as *prasad*. At Bhuteshwar, an ancient Shiva temple in Mathura, the floral offerings by devotees include fresh cannabis leaves. Bhang *lassi* and *bhang thandai* are popular during this season. The fresh green leaves and seeds of the cannabis plant are ground to a thick paste using a mortar and pestle. Then it is shaped into lemon-sized balls or *goli*s. For *bhang lassi*, one *goli* is mixed with one cup of yoghurt and sugar, whisked and strained through a sieve and served on crushed ice.

For *thandai*, the mixture is prepared separately. *Thandai* literally means that which cools. So the ingredients have cooling properties too. Melon seeds, poppy seeds, anise seeds, black peppercorns (to provide enough heat to balance the cooling ingredients), saffron, cardamom, rose petals and almonds are soaked and ground to a paste. For preparing

milk *thandai*, a tablespoon of the paste, sugar and cold milk are mixed together with crushed ice and strained through a sieve, and served, sometimes with a dollop of *malai* on top. *Bhang thandai* is made in a similar way, with or without milk. One tablespoon of *thandai* paste and one *goli* of *bhang* are mixed with a glass of water/milk, with ice and sugar, mixed well, and strained through a sieve or fine muslin cloth, and served. *Bhang thandai* is also the favourite drink during the festival of colours, Holi, when people shed inhibitions and have good time, with a little help from the intoxicating drink. Some members of the priestly community of Mathura, the Chaubeys, are known to consume it routinely as an appetizer.

Kachoris and Bedmis

*Kachori*s are a popular snack in the entire northern India. Packed with calories, savoury, hot and rich textured *kachori*s, stuffed with a spiced lentil paste, deep fried in *ghee*, are a delightful breakfast dish. Accompanied with a hot and spicy potato curry, the *kachori* tastes heavenly as an early morning meal. In Mathura–Vrindavan it is a popular breakfast of the masses, and gods alike. The deities are often offered *kachori* for *bhog*. The *kachori* and the curry are both tempered with *hing* (asafoetida), which aids digestion. The lentil is *urad* or *mung*, soaked overnight, ground to a coarse paste and spiced. The dough for *kachori*s is made from wholewheat flour or

refined flour, and kneaded with water with the addition of ghee and salt. To make a *kachori*, dough is pinched, stuffed with a lentil paste, sealed, flattened and rolled out by hand and deep fried in hot *ghee*. After it has puffed up to a crispy round ball, it is commonly served in plates made of dried leaves, along with a ladleful of spicy potato curry. A breakfast of *kachori*s and *jalebi* holds one up till lunch time.

The *bedmi*, another form of *kachori*, popular in the Braj region is an alternate breakfast. The dough for *bedmi* uses semolina for structure and crispness, mustard oil for the flavour and texture, and salt. The stuffing of ground *urad* dal, spices, *hing* and ginger is sealed in a dough ball which is rolled out thin and deep fried in *ghee*. The curry is made from boiled mashed potatoes, green chilli, peppercorns and ginger paste, salt and water, cooked in an iron *kadhai* which renders it a dark colour. No tomatoes are used, but some cooks add buttermilk or curd for tanginess. Most feasts and festivals in the Braj region have *bedmi* on their menu.

Pakoras

If there is a snack popular in any part of India, it is the *pakora* or fritters. Though it is a North Indian dish, it has a universal appeal owing to its versatility, ability to satiate hunger and ease of making. It is a favourite anytime snack in the temple streets of Mathura. Made by dipping green peppers, paneer, vegetables, or even sliced bread in a batter of chickpea flour, water and spices, and deep fried in hot mustard oil, it is served with mint and coriander chutney. Another form of *pakora* popular in the Braj region is the *ram laddoo* or *mung dal pakori*. It is made from soaked and ground *mung* beans, spiced with ginger coriander and green chillies. Small balls of this paste are dropped in hot oil and fried to a golden colour, and served hot with a green chutney. For pilgrims and travellers it is a go-to snack as it is readily available at train or bus stations, or off the streets, at any hour. During Holi, even *bhang pakoras* are served.

Visitors looking to sample street food in Mathura city will find plenty along the stretch between Chowk and Holi Gate on the old Agra Road.

Glossary

History of Mathura

Ahmed Shah Abdali: Ruler of Afghanistan from 1747–1772; He raided India several times through the Punjab, gaining notoriety for wanton destruction, loot and indiscriminate killings. He defeated a formidable Maratha army in the Third Battle of Panipat in 1761.

Aurangzeb: The last of the notable, powerful Mughal emperors. The expanse of the Mughal empire in India reached its zenith under his rule from 1658–1707. He was a controversial puritanical Muslim and iconoclast responsible for the destruction of Hindu temples and their replacement with Islamic structures.

Bhakti movement: Literally 'Devotional movement', the term refers to a mainly Hindu movement in medieval India to revive spirituality and spread religion among the masses using music, poetry in local languages and community chanting and prayers, from 7th to 17th century.

Delhi Sultanate: Name of the medieval Islamic empire that ruled northern parts of India between 1206–1526; includes the Khilji, Tughlaq and Lodi dynasties.

Dwapar Yug: Time, according to Hindu mythology and belief, is divided into 4 yugs (eras). The oldest era is *Satya Yug* or age of truthfulness, a golden period; the second and third eras viz. *Treta Yug* and *Dwapar Yug* are marked by a gradual decline in ethical values until the present era, called *Kali Yug*, when cruelty, materialism, lust and immorality prevail.

Jats: A rugged, traditionally agrarian community found mostly in the northern Indian states of Punjab, Haryana, eastern Rajasthan and western Uttar Pradesh, and Pakistan.

Magadh: An ancient kingdom centered around present-day Bihar in Eastern India.

Mahmud Ghazni: The 11th century Muslim ruler of the Ghaznavid Empire with its capital at Ghazni in Afghanistan. He is said to have invaded India 17 times during which he pillaged Hindu temples, most famously those of Mathura and Somnath.

Marathas: A Marathi-speaking warrior class from western India (present-day Maharshtra) whose greatest leader was Chhatrapati Shivaji (1630–1680).

Nav Ratnas: Translated as 'nine jewels', these were nobles of the royal court during Akbar's reign who were known to possess outstanding abilities in their respective fields.

Orchha: A town in the modern-day province of Madhya Pradesh, formerly a princely state.

Parikrama: The act of circumambulating a holy place in the hope of earning spiritual merit.

Sadak-e-Azam: The original name of the Grand Trunk Road which ran from Kabul in Afghanistan across the Gangetic plains of north India to Dhaka in Bangladesh.

Scindias: A Maratha dynasty that ruled from Ujjain and Gwalior in present-day Madhya Pradesh.

Sher Shah Suri: A powerful military strategist and administrator, he defeated the Mughal emperor Humayun in battle and for a short interlude ruled over India in the 16th century.

Stupa: A dome shaped shrine, usually containing relics of a respected Buddhist teacher.

Suraj Mal: A powerful leader of the Jats (1707–1763) who ruled from Bharatpur in the 18th century.

Tansen: One of the nine jewels of Akbar's court, Tansen was an outstanding musician and composer. He is credited to have invented several *raga*s or melodies of Indian classical music.

Legend of Shri Krishna

Alvar poets: 12 Tamil poets who lived between 6th–9th century CE. They were supreme devotees of Vaishnavism and responsible for its spread in the Tamil speaking regions of southern India.

Anjolie Ela Menon: A contemporary Indian artist based in Delhi, born in 1940.

Bala Saraswati: A leading exponent of Bharatanatyam who lived from 1918–1984. She was bestowed with India's second highest civilian award, the Padma Vibhushan, in 1977.

Basohli: A town near Jammu in north India, famous for its miniature paintings in the Pahari School style.

Bilhana: An 11th century Kashmiri poet, known for a long love poem of 50 stanzas called "Chaura Panchaskita" or the 'Love Thief'.

Bishnupur: A town in Bankura district of West Bengal, situated 138 km from Kolkata. It is famous for its terracota temples.

Cholas: A powerful dynasty that ruled many parts of southern India from the 10th to 13th centuries. Sculptures in bronze reached new heights of finesse during this period.

Guruvayur temple: An important Vishnu temple in Guruvayur town of Kerala state in southern coastal India. It famously accepts live elephants as offerings to God.

Gwalior and Benaras gharanas: North Indian (Hindustani) classical vocal music schools originating from Gwalior and Varanasi.

Haveli Sangeet: Devotional north Indian classical music in praise of Lord Krishna sung in temples, especially by followers of the Vallabhacharya sect. Said to have originated when temples were frowned upon by Muslim rulers and idols were worshipped inside homes *(havelis)*.

Jagannath Temple: Located in Puri city in the eastern state of Odisha, this is one of the holiest temples of Hindus dedicated to Jagannath, an incarnation Lord Vishnu.

Jayadev: 12th century poet from Odisha state who is known for his classic work *Geet Govind*, an epic poem about the romance between Krishna, Radha and the milkmaids of Vrindavan.

Kalamkari: A type of hand-painted textile from Andhra Pradesh.

Kalighat: A locality in Kolkata city with a famous temple of goddess Kali. It is the origin of a unique style of painting that developed in the 19th century.

Kangra: A district in the north Indian state of Himachal Pradesh, famous for miniature paintings of Krishna and Radha.

Kirtan: Devotional singing in a congregation.

Kummi dance: A folk dance of South India marked by women dancing in a circle.

Mirabai: One of the leading mystics of the Bhakti Movement in the 16th century who belonged to the royal family of Mewar, Rajasthan, she is known for her fanatical devotion to Krishna which is reflected in her poetry, written in a Rajasthani dialect of Hindi.

Mithila: A region in North Bihar, bordering Nepal.

Narayana Bhattathiri: A Sanskrit poet of Kerala who lived from 1560–1646. His magnum opus *Narayaneeyam* is a poetic interpretation of the Bhagwat Purana.

Narsinh Mehta: A 15th century saint of Junagadh in Gujarat state who is regarded as the first poet of the Gujarati language. He is the author of the hymn *"Vaishnav Jan To"* which was a favourite of Mahatma Gandhi.

Padmanabhaswamy Temple: A centuries-old temple of Lord Vishnu (Padmanabhaswamy) situated in Thiruvanantapuram, the capital of Kerala. Considered one of the richest endowed temples in southern India, it is patronised by the royal family of the erstwhile Travancore princely state.

Paithani: A town in Aurangabad district of Maharashtra, known for a particular design of sarees.

Raja Ravi Verma: One of India's greatest painters who lived from 1848–1906. He was the first to paint Indian themes and subjects in a European style.

Sopanam: A style of classical singing that developed in the temples of Kerala.

Swami Bilwamangala: A 9th century poet-devotee of Lord Krishna who hailed from South India.

Swathi Thirunal: The ruler of Travancore state from 1829–1846. He is considered a great poet, musician and composer of *ragas*.

Udupi: A town in south-west Karnataka, known for a large Krishna temple, chain of restaurants and as an educational hub.

Braj Bhasha

Amir Khusro: A versatile genius who lived from 1253–1325, Amir Khusro was a poet and musician who is believed to have invented among other things, the *sitar*.

Bihari: Born Biharilal Choubey, he was poet laureate in the court of Jai Singh, the ruler of Jaipur. He lived from 1595–1663 and his most famous work *Satsai* consists of 700 verses in Braj Bhasha, on the love between Radha and Krishna.

Harivansh: A prolific Braj Bhasha poet and Krishna devotee who lived from 1502–1552, he wrote under the penname 'Hit'. A contemporary of the first Goswamis of the Gaudiya sect, he broke away from them and formed his own Radhavallabh Sampraday which today is centered around the temple by the same name in Vrindavan.

Rahim: Abdul Rahim Khan-e-Khanan was one of the nine jewels in the court of Mughal emperor Akbar and one of his military commanders. Rahim who is best known for his *dohas* (couplets) on everyday life, also wrote devotional poetry in Braj Bhasha.

Raskhan: Born Syed Ibrahim Khan, this 17th century poet was educated in Persian and is believed to have translated the *Bhagwat Purana* into that language. Yet, he had a mastery over Braj Bhasha as is reflected in his devotional poetry on Krishna.

Surdas: Blind from birth, Surdas is a doyen of the classical poets who wrote in the Braj Bhasha language. A disciple of Vallabhacharya, the Bhakti period saint and devotee of Lord Krishna, Surdas lived from 1478–1583, mostly in Parsoli village near Govardhan.

Taj Bibi: Said to be one of the wives of Mughal emperor Akbar, Taj Bibi was a 16th century poet who wrote devotional poetry on Krishna in Braj Bhasha. She was a follower of Vitthalnathji, the son of Vallabhacharya.

Tulsidas: A revered Hindu saint and poet who lived from 1532–1623 in Varanasi. He is best known for the *Ramcharitmanas*, a retelling of the Sanskrit Hindu epic the *Ramayana* in the local Awadhi language, thereby making the story of Ram accessible to the masses.

A Kaleidoscope of Art and Culture

Angvastra: A simple stole with ethnic designs, traditionally hung over the shoulders by men.

Annakoot: A festival held shortly after Diwali, celebrating the rescue of the people of Govardhan from the wrath of Indra by Lord Krishna. Also known as Govardhan Puja.

Bhagwat Puran: Of Hinduism's 18 *Puranas*, this is the most widely read. Written around the 10th century CE, it is the single biggest source of the legends and lore associated with Krishna and Radha.

Bodhisatvas: A saintly person who is on the path to becoming a Buddha.

Braj Foundation: A charitable foundation in Vrindavan, engaged in the restoration of ancient temples, water bodies and other spots associated with Lord Krishna as well as reviving old cultural arts and crafts. Founded by the lawyer-activist Vineet Narain.

Chandragupta Maurya: The founder and head of a powerful empire of ancient India in the 4th century BCE with headquarters in Patliputra, modern-day Patna, in the east Indian state of Bihar.

Chunri: A long scarf worn by women on the Indian subcontinent.

Daan Lila: Another local festival related to the tale of Krishna demanding milk and cream as toll from maids passing through the Daan Ghati Valley in Govardhan.

Five Vrishni heroes: According to a stone inscription discovered in Mathura district dating to the 1st century CE, the five were Vasudeva-Krishna (Lord Krishna himself), Samkarshana (Balram), Pradyumna (Krishna's son), Samba (Krishna's son) and Aniruddha (Krishna's grandson). Some scholars believe they were ancient kings of the Mathura region who were deified for their heroic deeds.

Gandhara School of art: A school of art that flourished in the Gandhara (Kandahar) region of Afghanistan during 1 BCE–7 CE.

Gopashtmi: A local festival in Mathura in mid-November, when cows are worshipped.

Guru Sandeepan: The guru of Krishna and Balram, who taught them the Vedas and archery.

Janamashthmi: Anniversary of the birth of Lord Krishna. Celebrated in most parts of India and Nepal.

Kanhai Chitrakar: An indiginous artist of Mathura (1934–2013), Kanhai Chitrakar established a style of painting portraits embellished with gold leaves, gold paint and precious stones. He was awarded the Padma Shri in 2000.

Lehenga: A long skirt worn by Indian women , especially during ceremonies like weddings.

Megasthenes: Greek ambassador to the court of the Indian emperor Chandragupta Maurya in the 4th century BCE. He wrote the travelogue *Indica*, regarded as the first book by a Western writer on India.

Nathdwara: A pilgrim town in Southern Rajasthan famous for the Srinathji Temple of the infant Lord Krishna, which is the place of origin of Pichhwai paintings.

Panini: Sanskrit grammarian and scholar, author of *Ashtadhyayi* who lived around the 5th century BCE.

Patanjali: The author of many Sanskrit works including the *Yoga Sutras* who lived around the 3rd century BCE. Regarded as the father of Yoga.

Pichhwai: Folk art paintings on cloth originating in Nathdwara, Rajasthan.

Pitr Paksha: A 16 day period of abstinence, also known as *Shradh*, when Hindu families honour their deceased ancestors by offering prayers, food and water to their souls.

Raga: A concept central to Indian classical music. It is a collection of notes that are played or sung in a particular melodious formation. There are dozens of *raga*s and their variations.

Samkarshana: Another name of Balram, elder brother of Krishna.

Shahji temple: A large Krishna temple near Nidhivan, Vrindavan, named after its founders. Built in the 19th century, It is notable for its unique spiral pillars and Belgian chandeliers.

Sharad Poornima: Full moon day marking the beginning of the winter season. It is considered auspicious in India and much of south and southeast Asia.

Shringar: The dressing up or adornment of the idol of a god, goddess. Also refers to a woman's makeup.

Skanda: Hindu god of War, also known as Kartikeya.

Sri Vitthalnath: The younger son and spiritual successor of Vallabhacharya. He made Gokul the headquarters of the sect.

Srimad Bhagwat: A respectful way of mentioning the *Bhagwat Puran*.

Tanjore school of painting: A style of painting that originated in Thanjavur, a city in the southern Indian state of Tamil Nadu. The framed paintings are mostly of gods, goddesses, religious monuments and are marked by the use of gold foil and inlay of glass beads.

Tirthankaras: A concept central to Jainism, a *tirthankara* is one who has transcended the material world and become a spiritual teacher, showing others the path to overcome the cycle of death and rebirth. There are 24 *tirthankara*s of whom Mahavir was the last.

Visaka: A disciple of Gautam Buddha and, later, as a wealthy woman, one of his main patrons.

Vrishni: A martial clan in ancient India of the Yadu (Yadav) race, to which Krishna is said to have belonged.

Yakshas: A class of demigods equipped with magical powers, worshipped in ancient India along with nature spirits.

Zardozi: A style of embroidery using gold and silver thread.

Brajbhoomi

Aarti: Praying aloud, often in unison, while waving oil, camphor or incense-lit lamps before a deity. This ritual recalls an ancient Hindu practice of offering fire to the Gods.

Ashram: A retreat of a holy man or woman and a centre for religious practices.

Barsana: A town situated 40 kms from Mathura, said to be the birthplace of Radha, the consort of Krishna.

Caravanserai: Roadside resting place for long distance travellers.

Chhati Puja: A traditional prayer for a newborn's bright future done six days after birth.

Chhatris: Umbrella shaped pavilions, common in Hindu, Sikh and Islamic architecture.

Daan Ghati: An important temple of Govardhan located in a valley in the Giriraj Parvat.

Dauji: An affectionate name for Krishna's elder brother Balram.

Dharamshala - A rest house for pilgrims.

Doab: Land that lies between two rivers. The Indo-Gangetic doab is the flat, fertile land that lies between the Ganges and Yamuna rivers.

Dwarkadheesh: Literally meaning 'King of Dwarka', this is the name of the Krishna temple in Mathura, established and managed by the followers of the medieval Saint Vallabhacharya.

Gaudiya Vaishnavas: The sect of Krishna worshippers founded by Chaitanya Mahaprabu in Bengal.

Ghat: A spot on a river bank used for mooring boats, washing clothes, bathing or performing religious rituals. It usually has a platform with steps leading down to the river.

Giriraj Parvat: A sacred hill in the town of Govardhan around which the most popular parikrama in the Braj region takes place.

Haridas Sampradaya: Sect or followers of Swami Haridas, a great saint-poet-musician of the 16th century.

Holi Gate: A city landmark, this ornate gate was built in 1874 by the Mathura municipality. It lies on the main approach to the Dwarkadheesh Temple and Vishram Ghat, two of Mathura's most visited sites. It is also known as Tilak Dwar.

Huranga: This is the name given to the raucus celebration in Baldev town where Holi is basically a no-holds barred affair, played mainly with coloured water.

Indra: The Aryan god of war who also ruled the waters of heaven that caused rain. Stories of Indra are found in abundance in the Rig Veda.

Jali: Lattice work, common in Rajasthani and Islamic architecture.

Jharonka: Ornate window, often a part of North Indian architecture.

Kaliya: According to the story told in the Bhagwat Puran, Kaliya was a giant serpent who lived in the Yamuna river in Vrindavan and harrassed and terrified all those who passed by. Kaliya was subdued and killed by Krishna after a resolute battle.

Kanishka: The greatest of the Kushan kings who ruled over a vast empire extending from Central Asia to Mathura.

Kesi: According to the Puranas, Kesi was a demon sent by Kansa in the shape of a horse to kill the infant Krishna when he lived in Gokul. Kesi was destroyed by Krishna and Krishna is frequently referred to as Keshav—the slayer of Kesi—in the scriptures, including the *Bhagwad Gita.*

Kos: A measure of distance, now obsolete, with 1 kos equivalent to approximately 3 kilometers.

Kunj Vihari: Literally 'One who dwells in a garden', which was Swami Haridas' way of describing Lord Krishna.

Kushans: Headquartered around Kandahar, a region in modern Afghanistan, the Kushan empire flourished from the 2nd century BCE to 3rd century CE. Kushan art and dress was heavily influenced by Greek culture while their religion was Buddhism.

Mansi Ganga: A sacred water body in Govardhan.

Mathura School of Art: The Mathura School of Art flourished from the 1st to 4th century CE comprising predominantly of sculptures in mottled red sandstone ranging from figures of Yaksha (nature spirits) to exquisitely carved statues of Buddha, the Jain Tirthankaras and Hindu gods and goddesses.

Nagara: North Indian temple architectural style where the temple is typically built on a platform with steps leading up to it. There may be many towers but the main idol of worship is placed under the tallest. The lesser towers may cover the secondary idols or the hall for the congregation.

Padma Purana: One of eighteen Puranas or ancient sacred Hindu texts containing thousands of spiritual verses in Sanskrit.

Pashtuns: Also known as Pathans, they are a group of ethnic tribes with origins in North-west Pakistan and Eastern Afghanistan.

Pietra dura: Stone inlay work of Italian origin.

Ramanuja: A hugely influential Hindu philosopher-saint and social reformer from Tamil Nadu in South India who lived in the 12th century. He was at the forefront in the propagation of Vaishavism or worship of Vishnu. His ideas and teachings influenced the growth of the Bhakti movement.

Sadabad: A town in Hathras district of Uttar Pradesh which, for a short while, was the headquarters of Mathura district during British rule.

Samadhi: The memorial of an eminent person, usually where his/her ashes are interred.

Seven Goswami Temples: The seven temples of Lord Krishna estalished in Vrindavan by the first disciples of Chaitanya Mahaprabhu. These are the Madan Mohan, Govind Dev, Radharaman, Radha Damodar, Shyamsundar, Gokulanand and Gopinath Temples.

Shani Dev: A deity who is feared since his displeasure is believed to bring bad luck to a person. By propitiating him, fortunes can be reversed.

Shikhar: The main spire in North Indian temple architecture.

South Indian style temple architecture: Unlike the curved *shikhar*s of North Indian temples, South Indian Hindu temples have a rectangular pyramidical shape with a prominent entrance gate (*gopuram*). Though there is no one style of architecture, many temples and *gopurams* have a facade that is covered with miniature sculptures or shrines, depicting stories from the scriptures.

Tulsi: The holy basil plant, considered sacred by Hindus. It is often found planted in the courtyards of Hindu households.

Yajna: A vedic ritual done in front of a sacred fire accompanied by chants.

Yamuna: A river sacred to the Hindus because of its association with the Krishna legend. Originating in the Himalayas, it is a tributary of the Ganges which it joins at Prayagraj in central Uttar Pradesh.

Festivals and Parikramas of Mathura

Hiranyakashyap: The king of demons in Hindu mythology who subjected his own son Prahlad to an ordeal by fire. He was killed by Lord Vishnu in his half man-half lion incarnation.

Imli Tala: A spot on the banks of the Yamuna in Vrindavan, revered by the Gaudiya Vaishanavs, as Chaitanya Mahaprabhu is believed to have meditated here under a tamarind tree.

Jatras of Bengal: Travelling theatres that originally performed dance dramas on Krishna-centric themes in rural areas of Bengal.

Jhankis: Tableaus of sculptures or puppets representing religious figures or scenes.

Kansa Quila: A 16th century fort, now in ruins, on the banks of the Yamuna in Mathura. It was the site of an observatory built by Raja Man Singh of Jaipur in the 16th century.

Phoolwali Holi: Here Holi is played using flowers instead of colours. Usually performed on stage with trained dancers in the role of Krishna, Radha and the milkmaids.

Pichkaris: Hand-held water pistons, which are the traditional devices for sprinkling coloured water during Holi.

Potra Kund: A large water tank adjacent to the Krishna Janam Bhumi Temple in Mathura. It is believed that it was used to bathe the newly born Krishna by his mother Devaki.

Ashrams, Saints and other Famous Inhabitants, and Gaushalas

Awadhi: A dialect of Hindi, spoken in the Awadh region of central Uttar Pradesh.

Baiju Bawra: The popular name of Baijnath Misra, a legendary classical singer and contemporary of Tansen who lived in the 16th century.

Garuda Purana: One of the 18 holy Hindu texts called *Puranas*. Written around the 10th century, it is attributed to Sage Vyas. Traditionally, a recitation from this *Purana* is done for the peace of the soul of a deceased person.

Gayatri Mantra: A verse from the *Rig Veda*, often recited at sunrise and sunset as part of daily Hindu ritual.

Gayatri Parivar: Sect founded by Acharya Sriram Sharma whose teachings centred around chanting the Gayatri Mantra.

Hanuman: The monkey god of Hindus, widely worshipped as a remover of obstacles (*sankat mochan*). Stories of his deeds and miracles are also found in the *Ramayan*.

Jai Gurudev: A relatively recent guru with a mass following.

Karma Bhumi: Place of deeds.

Langar/bhandara: A charity kitchen, where food is served free of cost.

Ma Anandmayee: Regarded as a saint by her followers, Ma Anandmayee hailed from Bengal and is believed to have spiritual healing powers. Among her followers was former Indian Prime Minister, Indira Gandhi.

Machan: A raised platform, often constructed on a tree, usually used by hunters or bird watchers for spotting animals or birds.

Mahamantra: The chant composed by Chaitanya Mahaprabhu in praise of both Lord Krishna and Lord Ram.

Mata Sudevi: The adopted name of Friedericke Brunning, a German lady who runs the Radha Surabhi cow shelter near Barsana.

Nainital: A beautiful lake town in the Himalayas. Formerly a summer capital of the government of Uttar Pradesh.

Ram: Another incarnation of Lord Vishnu, Lord Ram is as widely worshipped in India as Krishna is. His story is told in the *Ramayan*, Hinduism's second epic (along with the *Mahabharata*) written by the Saint Valmiki.

Ramakrishna Mission: A prominent social service organisation in India, founded by the Hindu spiritual leader Swami Vivekananda with branches all over India and overseas. Offers spiritual guidance as well as charitable educational and health services.

Ramcharitmanas: A widely read version of the *Ramayana*, written in Awadhi by the saint-poet Tulsidas, who lived in the 16th–17th century.

Ramesh Baba: Born Rameshwar Prasad Shukla, he served with the Uttar Pradesh Police in Allahabad before settling down in Barsana where he founded what has grown into one of the largest shelters for cows in the country.

Rashtriya Swayam Sewak Sangh (RSS): A nationalist Hindu oganization founded in 1925 at Nagpur in Maharashtra state by K.B. Hegdewar. Among its objectives is to organise Hindu society by inculcating a spirit of discipline and patriotism from childhood. The RSS has millions of followers in India.

Sadhvi Rithambara: A vocal advocate of Hindu nationalism, Sadhvi Rithambara is a powerful orator and founder of Durga Vahini, the women's wing of the Vishva Hindu Parishad.

Saraswati Shishu Mandir: A chain of schools run by the RSS.

Sulabh International: Known for its work in environment sanitation, Sulabh International is a social service organisation founded by Dr Bindeswar Pathak. It has successfuly built thousands of public toilet facilities in different parts of the country.

Telegu: Name of the language spoken in the south Indian states of Telengana and Andhra Pradesh. Persons belonging to these states and speaking this language are also called Telegu.

Varanasi: One of the seven holy cities of India, situated in the state of Uttar Pradesh. Regarded as the oldest continuously inhabited city in the world.

Vedas: The oldest Hindu scriptures dating to the 2nd century BCE. Written in Sanskrit, they are four in number viz. the *Rig*, *Sam*, *Atharv* and *Yajur Veda*s. Their contents are said to be thousands of years old, passed down generations by oral tradition.

Cuisine of Mathura

Bhojanakutuhula: A 17th century compilation in Sanskrit of recipes and tips on consuming food, based on principles of Ayurvada.

Brahmand Ghat: Literally, 'universe ghat'. The main ghat on the Yamuna River at Gokul where, according to legend, the infant Krishna opened his mouth to reveal the entire universe encapsulated within it.

Charaka Samhita: An ancient authoritative text on Ayurvada, the Indian system of medicine, written in Sanskrit by Maharishi Charaka, a saint physician, who lived in the 5th century BCE.

Durga: Hindu goddess of strength, fertility and power who is the object of worship during Navratri.

Falahari: Literally, a fruit meal. Vegetarian meal cooked without spices except rock salt and without onions or garlic, commonly consumed on festival days.

Laxmi: The Hindu goddess of wealth.

Naivedya: Sanskrit word meaning 'offerings to God'.

Navratri: An auspicious period of 9 days which occurs twice a year.

Prahar: One-eighth of the day (three hours).

Satvik: The purest of the three personality types, *Satvik*, *Rajsik* and *Tamsik* as classified in Indian philosophy.

Vedic cooking: Cooking by aligning taste (sweet, sour, bitter, savoury, etc.) to the partaker's emotional constitution.

acknowledgements

The authors wish to acknowledge the contributions made by the following:

For giving us his in-depth explanation of the religious significance of Mathura and Vrindavan, we wish to thank Acharya Shrivatsa Goswami, the Gaudiya Vaishnav scholar, Indologist and high priest of the Radha Raman temple of Vrindavan;

Through his sermons, the priest of the Radha Raman Temple and religious orator Abhishek Goswami, gave us a glimpse of the cultural traditions of Braj as did Vineet Narain, the well-known legal activist-turned social crusader, through his writings and blogs;

We are also grateful to Krishn Kanhai, the elder son of Kanhai Chitrakar and doyen of the Kanhai school of Mathura paintings, for giving us free access to his art;

Shailja Kant Misra, the Vice Chairman of Braj Teerth Vikas Parishad and Nagendra Pratap, Vice Chairman, Mathura Vrindavan Development Authority provided invaluable assistance for us to visit different sites of the Braj region and observe the worthy work being done by the BTVP.

We are indebted to Shri Sanjeev Chopra for his guidance and support;

Pulkit Khare, the District Magistrate of Mathura and his staff, including Preeti Jain, Deputy Collector, proved to be of enormous help in getting access to various temples and other establishments of the twin cities;

We wish to express our appreciation to the National Archives of India, New Delhi, the Indian Museum, Kolkata and the Government Museum, Mathura for generously providing access to rare manuscripts and historical artefacts;

We wish to express gratitude to Hema Maliniji, celebrated actor, danseuse and popular politician of Mathura for sending her message for the book;

We also wish to place on record the exceptional photographic contributions of Lalit Rajora and Olivier Bernicat;

We extend our heartful thanks to the publisher Tultul Niyogi, editors Dr Nirmal Kanti Bhattacharjee and Anwesha Panda and designers Anushri Gupta and Shashi Bhushan Prasad for bringing this book to its fruition;

Finally, special thanks to the people of Mathura–Vrindavan—the street vendors, the temple priests, the weekend tourists, the *parikrama* pilgrims for generously sharing their experience of the holy land of Braj during our interactions with them.